Fresh Bread

From The Pastor's Table

*62 Loaves of "Fresh Bread" with
Life-Insights Being Discovered in More Than
50 Years' Pastoring*

by Joel S. McGraw

Xulon PRESS

www.xulonpress.com

Table of Contents

Endorsements

"Keep this book at your bedside! It is written with the maturity of an elder pastor-statesman. You will find it thought provoking, spiritually insightful, and sometimes humorous in its perspective of the twists and turns of life."

James Smith, M.Ed, D. Min
Lic. Professional Counselor, Retired
Huntsville, Alabama

"Tremendous! When I got this manuscript I could not put it down until I read it through."

Dr. Robert Spence
President, Evangel University
Springfield, Missouri

"Joel McGraw has done all of us a favor by giving us some *Fresh Bread*. This book is witty, humorous, practical, insightful and rock-solid theologically. It packs a punch for those of us who need to be regularly punched. Do yourself a special favor. Read this book. Do your friends a favor. Buy one for each – all of you will be richly blessed. Thanks, Joel, for some bread from Heaven."

James R. Eby, Founder/President
Mission Catalyst International
Houston, Texas

"Fresh Bread from this pastor's table has nourished his congregation for years. Like the loaves with which Christ fed the many, these few loaves will nourish all who partake. Here is profound wisdom in small tasty slices. Excellent writing and memorable life lessons."

James L. Daniels, Retired
Former Assistant to Dr. Werner von
*   Braun*
An Assistant to The NASA
*   Administrator*
Writer and Communications
*   Instructor*
Huntsville, Alabama

Introduction

How Come This Book

Most of my preaching years I have felt too young and inexperienced to have anything to say except in a defined preaching or teaching assignment. This has been especially true when I've been among other preachers. Then one day I was meeting with a large number of preachers from various church groups and realized I was the oldest person there.

I missed the day when I was the right age.So, what do I do? I choose and feel impelled to share a few practics I have learned and am learning in the trenches. I have learned that in church-life "shepherds" and "sheep" may have different functions, but we all have the same life-needs, and we can eat "Fresh Bread" together at the same table. I've been going back and eating some of those morsels. I think it must be like Samson of old returning and eating honey out of the carcass of a lion that sought to destroy him earlier.

Most of what I share has been uncovered at the end of a fast. I have a special place for those end-of-the-fast times, a table that we call the "break-fast" table. Most of my fasts are short, but at the end of each is where I have my clearest thinking and my best communication with God. Most days, starting sometime between 4 a.m. and 6 a.m., I am alone at my "break-fast" table for one to three hours. That is an unrushed time with God. I seldom get a phone call during that time, and the Lord hardly ever prompts me to call others at that time.

With my Bible, two or three resource books, and prayer I sincerely believe I hear from God. It is there I see events of my yesteryears and their meanings more clearly. Many years ago I heard myself praying, "Father God, please help me not to misunderstand what I don't yet understand."

In the following pages I share with you sprigs of what have seemed delayed understandings. These are lessons I wish I could have better learned, and more effectively applied earlier. As I write this it seems that I'm hearing, "I tried to teach you but you were too distracted and unreceptive to learn."

This "Fresh Bread" is a collage of 62 substantive life survival elements which are also life nourishment I have experienced along the way. All have proven genuine in the "field tests" of God's Truth in real life. Most have been tested in my own life. Each "loaf" was written and printed earlier in bulletins at Faith Chapel under "Shepherd's Sharing" and "Fresh Bread from Pastor's Table." These have been selected from several hundred and grouped together for this publication.

As I have personally read back through these "life related accounts" I have been fed and refreshed all over again. Though minimally "chewed" for you, I see clearly now how this "Fresh Bread" has repeated backgrounds of battles, hunger, trials, temptations, hurts, disappointments, flat places, and other needs through which God was bringing me.

This book is written with prayer that many will read these pages, hear with their hearts, and benefit in the real issues of daily life. These are far more than "lessons." This is a "Life

Message." May you find a few coals of fire that will help better light your way, and from which you will find some warmth for your journey through this cold world.

Pastor Joel S. McGraw
Huntsville, Alabama

Dedication

To Janelle Barbee McGraw, the lady of my life, who has shown to me in real life the application of these lessons while I have been learning them. She has been there as my partner in life and ministry for more than 50 years.

Two Who Must Get Married

Here's a thought on getting life together and how to avoid falling apart.

I can pretty well guarantee a couple a wedding; not an individual, but a couple. I cannot guarantee anyone a marriage!

Today I must tell you of two who must get married, or there is going to be chaos. I'm talking about Creed and Deed, your creed and your deed. They are not twins, but partners. They must get married.

Everyone is comprised of *mystical* and material parts, your creed and your deed. One is invisible, almost indefinable. The other is very visible, and obvious to everyone. It may be what the Bible calls faith and works. Faith without works is dead, the Bible says. You probably know that works without faith will kill you. So there's death when there is either without the other.

But, back to this marriage thing: I'm talking about more than a wedding. The marriage that must be is the marriage of Creed and Deed.

Being converted, born again, is sort of like a wedding. Becoming a practicing disciple of Jesus Christ is sort of like a real marriage.

I tell couples that weddings don't last, but marriages do, or they are supposed to. The wedding only lasts for a few minutes, or hours at the most. The marriage is to continue, ever developing, maturing, and improving.

Being born again happens. You aren't and then you are.

Becoming a practicing disciple of Jesus Christ is sort of like a marriage. It is an ongoing process ever developing.

You can subscribe to the Apostles Creed, the Nicene Creed, the Articles of Faith, or some other crisp statement of the basics of the Christian faith. But the more accurate declaration of your real belief is spelled out in your deeds, your behavior.

Your creed is what you say you believe. How does your creed pan out in your daily deeds? Do you behave your belief?

I believe people do behave their real belief. Oh, I know, behavior may not line up with the creed we read. But what we really believe is declared by our deeds, our works. I used to say to newcomers in church, "If you want to know what we really believe, do more than read the creed. Watch us. Hang out with us. The way we live, act, behave, drive, treat one another, handle disagreements, talk to strangers, respect and honor God...." That is how to know what we really believe.

You may want to do some self-examination. In fact, God's Word tells us to do exactly that.

The two who must get married then, are your spoken creed and your life deed out there in the world. I have been re-examining the marriage in my own life between Creed and Deed. The closer they get to one another the more love, joy, and peace they have in their home, me.

In fact, when you have the right creed really married to the matching deed of life you can expect a gracious family of children whose names will be Love, Joy, Peace, Patience, Kindness, Goodness, Faithfulness, Gentleness, and Self-control! (Galatians 5:22-23)

Just a wedding of Creed and Deed? There you get some kind of lopsided schizophrenia. You don't want to go there. Settle for nothing less than marriage!

Had Your Value
Appraised Lately?

Well, have you? Not your property, but your value, your worth. It will help you not to live on this world's "bargain counter" and be taken so easily.

I've noticed that many people reach for the highest appraisal on their property, but settle for the lowest appraisal of themselves.

Several years ago I read that the value of an average man was $2.35. Prices have gone up now to more than $15. That is the basic value of the various minerals and other stuff in your body.

There was a time when property, land, was limited to little more than the value of the dirt. So people devalued something by calling it "dirt cheap." No longer does that emphasize the low cost of something.

What about you? Oh, I know your body parts are of great value now for transplants. Some people have been known to sell some of their blood for quick cash. Others so graciously will donate a kidney to extend and enhance the quality of another person's life. The person receiving that kidney places inestimable value on that one part of another.

How much is all of who you are worth?

The devil and his representatives are the source of low value people put on themselves. I understand one factor appraisers use in appraising property has to do with how much someone else had paid for that property. Furniture appraisers pay a lot of attention to who designed and who made that furniture.

In case you have been considering a low appraisal on yourself, let me give you a point or two to consider.

One: Take note of your Designer/Maker. You are not the result of some fluke accidental assemblage of body parts, nervous system, intellectual intrigue, and spiritual quest. You are here by design and purpose. When you were born, God did not say, "Oops!"

Two: "You were bought with a price," the Bible says, "Therefore glorify God with your body and your spirit which are God's." God has made optimum investment in you! You glorify God by obeying Him.

You have great value! Your value is not limited to the material substances in your body. Your value is far more than what you know, whom you know, or what you can do. Those are the areas by which many people are known. You are worth more than that!

Have you updated your appraised value lately?

Take a fresh look at God's high appraisal of you. Accept it! Believe it! Find inspiration and strength to live accordingly!

Before Jesus performed any miracles or gave the Sermon on the Mount, Father God said, *"This is my beloved Son in whom I am well pleased!"* God's value on His Son was not earned.

God's value on you is not earned. Your value is set by God Himself. God not only loves you, He likes you. He delights in you. He loves you, likes you, and delights Himself in you so much that He will go with you and enable you to become everything He has created you to be.

When you "be" all He wants you to be, then you can "do" all He wants you to do!

So take heart! Find your appraised value, not on the "bargain counter" of this world, but under the price tag our Lord has paid!

Other People's Surprise Behavior: Why?

People still seem to be surprised and even shocked at the aberrant behavior of others. Take a look in two places – the mirror on the wall, and the mirror in God's Word, the Bible.

The surprise behavior of an astronaut as reported some time ago was equaled only by the many quick explanations by partially informed "professionals" and other people! The quick sensational salivation of the media's reporting "done-deal" details was little surprise.

When the stunning news began breaking of that astronaut's arrest, I immediately recalled words I read years ago – "The moment anyone comes to believe he is not capable of committing the most heinous sin, that moment he becomes the greatest fool in the world."

I listened to bits and spurts of extreme behavior related to that apparent "lust triangle." One "professional" said the cause of that berserk behavior was due to having reached the zenith of achievement and aspiration by flying in a very successful mission. The explanation was that some other extreme deed had to be done.

Another explanation had to do with the stress caused by her dual responsibilities of family along with her highly demanding work.

So? Many astronauts have families. How about all the others who also reached their aspiration?

The same day I heard that gripping news I had just read words from Oswald Chambers in his book, <u>Daily Thoughts For Disciples</u>. He said, *"...we are not prepared to accept Jesus Christ's diagnosis of the human heart...we* refuse the diagnosis of the only Master there is of the human heart!" Jesus said, *"Out of the heart come evil thoughts, murder, adultery, sexual immorality, theft, false testimony, slander."*

I run into people regularly who are surprised by the aberrant behavior of someone they know. In fact, some have been jolted by slices of their own behavior. Come to think of it, I blush now at some inappropriate things I have thought, done and said through the years. God's disfavor goes far beyond the few glaring and blatantly publicized criminal sins. Thankfully, by God's grace and help, I have not plummeted!

So what now?

Be alert! Surrender your life and behavior to God and His Word through Christ Jesus. Read again and digest Proverbs 3:5, *"Trust in the Lord with all your heart and lean not on your own understanding."*

Help rescue those who've been overcome. Jesus Christ gave His life to *"Rescue the perishing, care for the dying."* Let's line up with Him! We'll have fewer jolting surprises and be better prepared to deal with the aberrant (spelled s-i-n) behavior in ourselves and others.

Here's an idea that will help some. Chambers wrote that every Christian needs to be freed from the *"tyranny of moods and the tyranny of feelings he is not understood."* He said, *"Half the misery in the world comes because one person demands of another a complete understanding, which is absolutely impossible. The only Being Who understands us is the Being Who made us."*

Grab-hook Evangelism
vs. God's Way

Helping others know God is more than a method. It's a way!

The Church stands tall when touching others with a God kind of care! That means touching others with God. You do remember, "God is love."

"Grab-hook" evangelism has to do with using almost any tactic to get a quick verbal agreement from people to say, "Yes." It is sort of a "love'em and leave'em" method, statistical steeple chasing.

A guest from an undisclosed Muslim' country, told us the most effective way to reach Muslims for Christ is to "be genuine yourself" as you help them have an encounter with God in His goodness.

"Well," I said to him, "It seems to me you have found the best way to lead any people anywhere to Christ!"

I believe that is God's way of the most effective evangelism. Oh, I know, sometimes it's a "rescue the perishing" quick act! But the kind of winning people to your God that really helps them become disciples of Jesus is the kind where they see your genuinely caring Christianity in their encounter with your God.

Church, I have seen you open your arms, your hearts, your houses, your vehicles, your kitchens, and your speech to say, "God loves you and we do too!"

A few weeks of several deaths brought people from far away places and from across town. Dear ones, you have met them all with LOVE!

Leonard Sweet in his book, Carpe Manana, summed up a bit of real Christian history with:

"The world is a better place because:

"Michelangelo didn't say, 'I don't do ceilings.'

"A German monk named Luther didn't say, 'I don't do doors.'

"An Oxford don named John Wesley didn't say, ' I don't do fields.'

"Moses didn't say, 'I don't do rivers.'

"Noah didn't say, 'I don't do arks.'

"Mary Magdalene didn't say, 'I don't do feet.'

"Paul didn't say, 'I don't do letters.'

"Jesus didn't say, 'I don't do crosses'."

And, I might add, this local church didn't say, "I don't do bread, I don't do salad, I don't do beans, I don't do chicken, I don't do cake, I don't open my doors, I don't make midnight rides for others, I don't take off work, I don't......"

God's Word says, "Faith without works is dead." This church's faith is not dead!

Thanks, Church, we may be entering life-related evangelism that will do far more than make a few converts. Jesus said, "Go make disciples."

We are going for less "grab-hook" evangelism and more life-related! We believe this is God's way for us!

Welcome into the family!

For Prayer Results, Pray

That means we must do more than just pray around a little. It means we must pray! Let me share some help in stimulating and activating your prayer-life.

We are talking about more than just _saying_ our prayers. This is a call to ourselves and one another to _pray_ God-prayers.

Someone said it means **PUSH - P**ray **U**ntil **S**omething **H**appens!

Sometimes I yawn when I <u>say</u> my prayers. In fact, I have even gone to sleep _saying_ my prayers. I am beginning to understand why.

It has to do with the anatomy of the prayer.

When it is just a "gi'me, do-it" prayer and the request is the subject of my praying I get overwhelmed. I get disconnected. Then I tend to drift off somewhere else.

When I am the subject, my prayer tends to become ingrown and so painful or boring until my prayer circuit throws a breaker. In that disconnect I drift off or find myself unable to find words to keep going. At that point, if I'm still awake, I do remember one prayer word, "Amen," so I say it, end, and become less interested in praying again.

Let me tell you what I'm learning and practicing. God, in Christ, is the Subject of real prayer and the one praying is the first object followed by whatever else may be on or may come onto the prayer list. If it's *my prayer I can say it*. When it is *a God prayer I must pray it*.

You know who the Great Intercessor is, don't you? Sure, you got it! Jesus Christ ever lives to intercede for us in perfect sync with the will of Father God. God's Word says if we ask anything according to God's will He hears us and if He hears us we have the petitions for which we pray.

It is God's will that we get beyond "prayer roulette." Just praying around won't cut it. It is time we pray for results!

Here's how it works. My prayer must be to change me, the pray-er. It is basically praying, "It's me, it's me, it's me, oh Lord, standing in the need of prayer."

The *First Result*, God becomes the Subject of my praying. It's all about Him, Who He is, His will, His way. As I talk to God in my praying I learned to rehearse from Scripture things He has said and done in the past. I learned this information by reading the Bible, attending Sunday School, listening to Bible preaching, and hearing prayer warriors pray. In prayer I reference what He has said. I recall His work in my life and others I know. My hope rises. Divine inspiration begins to percolate all through me. Faith is activated and becomes substantive!

I find myself getting so aligned and in sync with God that I then know by revelation the more perfect will of God regarding myself and the matters for which I am praying. That's when I, the object, get in line with God in Jesus Christ, the Subject. The Holy Spirit then becomes the active verb guiding, sometimes gliding, the prayer.

Results? ***Prayer Results*** beginning with God as the Subject, then the pray-er and all else becoming like God

The ***Prayer Results*** of your family, your church, or your nation will be the composite Prayer Results of you and the others. Talk with someone else about this. Pray!

Sin is Abnormal: Be Normal

Did you hear about the boy who said, "I'm going to be different! I'm going to do what everybody else is doing!?" A man had a homemade yardstick. He had a lot of fun with it. He didn't tell others it was homemade. Another man measured a distance and said it was nine yards. Then the homemade-yardstick-man measured and said it was only six yards. Result? Confusion!

I once knew a homemade-holiness-man who had his own set of beliefs for his measurement of other people. He had even personally prayed to get saved, but he missed becoming a disciple of Jesus Christ. With his yardstick he began measuring others and found none who were the right length. In fact, he finally did a measurement on himself and found that he too came up short.

So what did my homemade-holiness-friend do? He decided the whole idea of holiness, righteousness with God, even being a Christian, was abnormal. So he chunked the whole idea and went in pursuit of "extreme normality." You know, if sinning is normal then sin a lot and be really normal.

What am I trying to say?

Our norm is not this world's norm. The world's norm keeps changing anyhow.

I can remember when "girls who didn't wear lipstick, boys who didn't curse, smoke, and chew or run around with girls who do, and all of them who didn't go to moving picture shows were considered Christians." Did I say that? What odd length yardsticks!

It is easier to please God than it is to please other people. That means it is easier for me to please God than it is to please you, and it is easier for you to please God than it is to please me.

Oh, but you say, Jesus said, "Be perfect even as your Father in heaven is perfect." You're right. That's what He said.

You know what will mess up a piece of equipment worse than anything else? Failing to service it, maintain it, use it, and repair it according to the designer's and manufacturer's instructions! That's what!

You know what? Do you know the way to mess up a person's life worse than anything else? Sure! You are picking right up on the idea.

Rules with do's and don'ts in the Bible are not to kill your joy. They are guidelines for your greatest fulfillment in life. The enemy told Eve that God's restrictions were meant to harm her. She bit it. She paid. We are still biting and paying.

God's Word tells of a life ruled not by homemade yardsticks, stoic regulations, or even opinion polls. God, our Creator, Redeemer, and Sustainer gives new birth with a new heart made normal again. In this renewed normal life it is no longer a tit for tat struggle, but an open arena of freedom from the abnormal.

My good friend who died not long after I was born, Oswald Chambers, wrote about the *"...natural instinct of the supernatural life of God within me...."* He said *"...sanctification (righteousness) is based on the way God has made us. When we are born again we become natural for the first time; as long as we are in sin we are abnormal, because sin is not normal."*

This is not do-it-yourself stuff I am talking about. Becoming and being a real Christian is not a self-improvement fad. This is a relationship with God wherein the Christ Himself lives and releases His life inside the Believer!

I dare you. I challenge you. Don't settle for this world's abnormality!

Get normal! Live normal! That's God's plan and God's enablement"

The Word is "Our:" Listen

"You" means you, not me.
"Me" means me, not you.
"Our" means you and me; "us," not just you or just me.
Church, for us, the word is "our;" all of us.
Here's an additional truism:
Holy God means God, not you, not me, not even us.
You, me, us, means you, me, us. There's more.

Church means Holy God AND Redeemed people, not just God and not just Redeemed people. By all means, Church is not a building.

Church, the word is "our," God and Redeemed us, we!

Remember, "we" is not spelled "w e e." "Wee" means very small, tiny, just a little bit. Any part of us without each other and Holy God in us should be spelled "w e e."

The word is "our," all of Redeemed US and Holy God. Then wee becomes WE!

The church is not wee. The church is we. It comes out, "our." This is the hour for "our" calling "us" to obey God in all "we" shall do.

A father and mother had to make a tough family decision. They were divided. She said this is what must be done. He got upset. It was an awesome matter with a "wee" resource to deal with it. Then God moved in and "wee" became "we." God said to Father Abraham, "Don't get upset, let it not be grievous unto thee. Listen to what Sarah is saying." God assured them as they obeyed Him that He would be in charge of the outcome.

One veteran Christian wrote, "The dilemmas of our personal life with God are few if we obey and many if we are willful."

Jesus Christ said, "As the Father taught me, I speak these things." He said, "I am nothing on my own but say only what the Father taught me...I always do what pleases Him..."

Oswald Chambers points out, "The secret of our Lord's holy *(right)* speech was that He habitually submitted His intelligence to His Father...our Lord had within Himself the Divine remembrance that every problem had been solved in counsel with His Father before He became Incarnate...the one thing for Him was to do the will of His Father, and to do it in His Father's way."

It is so difficult for some of us to get beyond the zone of our own life-box, so we simply "stay in the narrow grooves of our own experience, become specialists in certain doctrines and Christian oddities, but never become really God-like."

Remember the word is "our," not just you or me or God alone. He is the now-God who encompasses all of what we call "past" and all of what we call "future." Let's include Him; well, let's include us. He will deal with all our past and give us assurance for all our future, including every resource needed for now.

So church, the word is "OUR," not just God alone; not just you or any one, or even all of you. The word is certainly not "I," "me" or "my."

The word is "our." When God so graciously includes you and me our Church then becomes what God, you and I make it with each of us believing, praying, giving, forgiving, and serving in God's order and guidance.

This is the hour, the word is "our!" Let's roll!!!

There's a Call. Please Answer!

Check the I.D. Be sure you know who is CALLING! A long time ago John W. Swails, Bible Professor at Emmanuel College, taught us young preachers that preaching is not a profession and not a vocation. He said it is a call. That may be one reason why so many don't know what to do with us.

Some accountants won't do taxes for preachers. Where do we fit in?

But back to the call, what is it? At Emmanuel I was so enamored with God's call for me until evidently I missed much that I should have learned. Back then I was aware of only one call and two or three sub-calls. I knew about the call to "preach" and that some preachers were called to pastor, be missionaries, or evangelists. Period.

Now I believe God has a call for everyone. Each call has a mixture of God-designed giftings that make each of us different from all others who may have the same dominant call. All teachers are not identical. All evangelists are not alike. No pastor is just like any other pastor. None with a call in administration is the same as any other administrator. Yet, each is called. Do you get the drift?

All who serve in God's calling have varying levels of zest, courage, and focus. Some seem to be more consistently encouraged and others seem to struggle with gloom a mighty lot. Remember, this applies to all with a call. I am talking about every role where people serve the Lord – ushers, greeters, singers, preachers, bookkeepers, evangelists, helpers in whatever.

1) Do you know God's call for you?
2) Are you answering God's call for you?
3) Do you have too many downs?
a) Be sure it is God's call. There are helps on how to know.
b) There is a place, area of ministry, where you can be fulfilled in obeying God's call. Ask. It may be where God has no one serving right now. It may be where others are praying for God to send someone. Ask.
c) About downs. I have found help. Let me share.

Avoid prayer-roulette – be sure God, not the need or yourself, is the subject. Here is a similar truth about the call. In your call are you first serving God, or are you first serving the need? Needs yo-yo. Needs take away. God gives. Needs empty. God empowers.

When you are need-called and that need is, or appears to be met, then your mission is complete, your call is ended, and your purpose is gone. When you are God-called and a need is met, or the mission appears to fail, then your call remains steady, filled with purpose, awaiting God's next assignment.

We must be careful not to worship the need or the method. Many times people seem to worship their ideas and God is looked upon as only a blessing machine for humanity. The need must never become the call.

Jesus Christ faced all He faced and did all He did, even dying on the cross, because obedience to the will of His Father always came first. He gained inspiration and "up" by "I delight to do thy will." Jesus also declared to His disciples,

"Even as the Father has sent me, so send I you." Our call is to remain faithful to God in and beyond all the machinery of our civilization, in the midst of material prosperity, and in the time of crushing defeat."

We must never put people's needs or success first, nor should even a "passion for souls" exceed our "passion for Christ."

Have you heard the call? Be sure it is God's, not yours, or some overwhelming need! You will find your help from the source of the call!

Resurrection, a Call
for Cohabitation

All right, get up! Trust me. Get your head together. Look it up.

"Co" means together. "Habitation" means dwell. Cohabitation simply means dwell together. Unfortunately people have sexualized it to mean to live together as husband and wife, but unwed. What a shame. Another great word has become depraved!

By the way, reliable studies are now showing the disastrous results of unwed cohabitation including the decreased likelihood of a successful marriage afterward. But that is not what this call for cohabitation is all about. Read on.

Resurrection, a call for cohabitation? You heard me correctly. I am writing this a week after Easter. But we are not a week after resurrection. Resurrection was, but also is. It was a historical fact. But resurrection continues like an active verb in the present perfect continuing tense. Christ _IS_ Risen!

Remember Jesus asking Mary Magdalene, *"Dear woman, why are you crying? Who are you looking for?"* You may not actually remember, but you may remember reading about it in John 20.

41

Sit up. Mary was crying about, and looking for the dead body of Jesus. Eerie? Has our faith gotten much further?

I remember the Sunday after Easter, 1956. I was pastoring in Coalburg just north of Birmingham. After morning worship we all loaded up our cars and went for a picnic up at Cullman. One of our points of interest was a small chapel where my mind and spirit tried to grapple with the sight of a life-sized replica of the wounded, dead body of Jesus slumped across the lap of His mother, Mary. My soul staggered with the crosswinds of confusion.

Before Jesus' question to Mary Magdalene, she had already been asked, "Why are you looking among the dead for the living?" She just didn't get it.

Now, here we are. Easter, a week ago, high attendance – people recommitted their lives to God – miracles abounded. Casual observers missed much of what God did, but those who recognized the resurrected Christ who still lives, are still continuing to celebrate His resurrection!

What does all this have to do with calling for cohabitation? Here's my answer: most people don't want to dwell with a dead body. I believe that is about as much as many people perceive Christianity to be. So go back to the Word of God.

God's Word says, *"He that dwelleth in the secret place of the Most High, shall abide under the shadow of the Almighty."* (KJV) That sounds like Godly cohabitation to me, not with a dead body, but with the living God who gives all those "cohabitation promises" in the rest of Psalms 91.

So? Since Christ is God alive making Himself accessible to all of us let's do more than pray for a visitation from Him. Let's give way to more in our faith than living with a dead body.

Hey Church everywhere! Hey you! Let's settle with nothing less than dwelling together with Him and He with us! It is legal and right, made so by the death, burial, and resurrection of Jesus Christ!

Resurrection! It's a call for Godly cohabitation!

Man With A Floating Anchor

There's a reason "floating anchor" sounds silly. It is.
A floating anchor does have advantages. It is lightweight and easy to move around. It does not hang onto roots and stuff. A floating anchor allows your boat to move in any direction at anytime. You also can always see it.

However, there are reliable advantages of a fixed anchor. A fixed anchor will prevent your boat from drifting in unpredictable directions. A fixed anchor will disallow a slight wind or small water current to relocate you. Another advantage of a fixed anchor – are you ready? – when you catch that big one you can stick to your purpose and not be so fishy as being pulled to another position by the fish.

Floating sounds like activity with multiple options. In fact, it sounds rather risky. There's a reason it sounds that way. It is.

A fixed anchor is not only right for your boat; it works in life also. Here's an example. Leave it to small children to teach us. Two, three, and four year olds can learn and practice right behavior when the options are removed. The youngsters I know get into the van, go straight to their car seat, and either fasten their own seat belt or insist that it be fastened. They do it without a whimper or argument. They have learned there are no options. The fixed anchor in place holds.

Could this be what God's Word is getting at in Romans 6? *"Count yourselves dead to sin but alive to God in Christ Jesus."*

God's plan for all of us is no more floating anchors. We have a fixed anchor. God's part is in place. All that will ever be offered in redemption is already available. Jesus said, "It is finished."

We initiate nothing. God has provided in Christ all we will ever need. Now our part is to respond to what He has already done.

You cannot come up with a better plan. Chunk every floating anchor. Remove every option. None of them will ultimately give more than disappointment.

God's Word directs us to "Gird up the loins of our minds." Evidently that is something we can do, else God would not direct us to do it. I think it means to cut out the options, do away with the "floating anchors," and stick only with the fixed anchor in life.

The Apostle Paul said, *"This one thing I do..."* That was not a floating anchor.

Let's pull up the old Gospel song, sing it, and mean it:

> *I've anchored my soul*
> *In the haven of rest,*
> *I'll sail the wide seas*
> *No more;*
> *The tempest may sweep*
> *O'er the wild, stormy deep,*
> *In Jesus I'm safe evermore.*
> *A floating anchor is still silly.*

A floating anchor in life is also silly. There silly is spelled s i n f u l.

So, dear ones, be anchored! Be blessed!

"Consinsual" Activity:
Deal With It!

I t is difficult to be a maximum Christian all by yourself. Other people, of necessity, are involved.

It is also difficult to sin to the max all by yourself. Even sinning alone affects others, but sinning in a big way really involves others.

I need a new word to try and say what I see here, so the new word is "consinsual." Let's talk about it.

I know. The word consensual has to do with a mutual consent, or agreement by two or more regarding a specific decision or activity. It usually is closely associated with something sensual. Consensual is often used to try and make a wrong less wrong by proving that the one accused had the agreement of the one accusing, for instance in a rape trial.

"Consinsual" has to do with any sin committed in and with the agreement and participation of another. Sinning together is what I am trying to say. How do you deal with it? You can't get out of it all by yourself.

Assume the "consinsual" behavior was also criminal and one of the participants is caught and convicted. What happens to the other? When all the facts are in he is likely to be convicted also against his will. All of that spells t-r-o-u-b-l-e!

47

Here's another approach. Both boys agreed to steal a radio. They exited the building undetected and one of them said to the other, "That was not only illegal, but my dad taught me it is also a sin." The other one says, "I agree." They both had an inner conviction and decided to carry the radio back and confess. They did. Chances are the store manager would thank them, exonerate them and it may all be over.

However, if one of the boys was caught or even confesses, you had better believe the other one will be in hot water also.

Now, dealing with *"consensual"* behavior, you're in it together. The way out all the way calls for "together" again. Else, when one confesses and repents, he must somehow include in someway his "consinsual" constituents.

Sometimes dealing with the "consinsual" calls for restitution like paying debts and restoring what was stolen. Zacchaeus, after turning to Jesus, offered to give half his wealth to the poor and give back to those he had cheated in taxes four times what he had taken.

The best word I can think of right now in dealing with "consinsual" behavior is another "together" word, compassion. That is more than passion. Passion without a harness can be like a wild horse. Compassion is you indwelt with Christ's passion. It is Godly passion, pure in action and motive. Compassion has healing, restoration, and renewal in it, all for the good of the other.

"Consinsual" behavior is sinning together in agreement. Deal with it like all sins are dealt with. Confess with your mouth the Lord Jesus, and believe in your heart that God has raised Him from the dead. Confess your sins to Christ and He will cleanse you from all iniquity. Repent!

Take the initiative with or without the consent of your "consinsual" cohorts. Who knows? One or more of them may take the initiative and you will be forced to deal with it one way or another anyway. After all, God's Word says the time will come when every knee shall bow and every tongue confess that Christ is Lord.

From wherever you are, the way out is UP!

Find Freedom in "Co-independence"

Finding freedom in "Co-independence" means, finding freedom with someone else who is finding freedom.

America's big patriotic holiday is "The 4th." July 4, is known as Independence Day. It is the birthday of the United States of America. We have every right to celebrate! The life of America for more than 200 years has been splashed with mistakes of shame and sins of various degrees. The list seems to change every four or eight years, depending on who's monitoring the others but above it all we have reasons to celebrate!

Mistakes must be faced and dealt with regardless of size, shape, or form. Probably at the top of our list of sins is the sin of dealing with other's sins rather than our own. The irony of such activity is that the sins of others are not dealt with so much as they are advertised with Pharisaic, better than thou, pride.

By the way, America has more dimples than warts, more rights than wrongs, and more strengths than weaknesses. There are still Godly men and women in government, classrooms, science labs, engineering offices, law enforcement, sales floors, and even churches!

Now, back to freedom and "co-independence!"

On July 4, 1776, America became independent from Great Britain, but not independent overall. In fact, in those days and for many years thereafter our leaders, including our presidents, recognized our dependence upon God and often led prayers and called on the people to pray.

To find real freedom we must, as a nation and as individuals, find our freedom not in total independence, but in "co-independence." We must be independent of any outside force or inside perverse control. In order to do that, it is imperative that we be "co-independent." Together with God and others of like independence, we become dependent upon God and one another.

Raw independence is sin, the very essence of sin. *"All we like sheep, have gone astray; we have turned everyone to his own way;" (Isa. 53:6)* Thank God that Scripture does not end there. He continues, *"and the Lord has laid on Him the iniquity of us all."*

This is not co-dependence. That has to do with someone supporting another who is in bondage to the point where the supporting one comes into bondage to their need to be needed.

As a nation we need God and we need "one-another nations" of like vision and value! God's call for us not to be *"unequally yoked"* is more than a call for couples in marriage not to be unequally yoked.

The greatness and strength of America is the summation of the greatness and strength of the citizens of America. Everybody knows couples in marriage are not to be equally identical. They have complimentary but not divisive differences.

Fellow citizens, let us celebrate our complimentary differences, our "co-independence," and together in our common values and vision, find our greatness and strength!

Church, in Christ is our freedom. Let us celebrate our complimentary differences, "co-independence," and together in our common values and vision, find our greatness and strength!

You will find your greatest personal freedom not in your isolated raw independence, but in your "co-independence" with others. Your point of reference is Almighty God in the person of Jesus Christ. As both of us get closer to Him we will automatically get closer to one another.

Herein is our greatest freedom: with one another as American citizens – "co-independent" with others of like values and vision – "co-independent" as believers with God and one another! Celebrate!

...to Say at Your Funeral

Pardon me for bringing this up, but it's coming up anyhow. Let's get the jump on it. We all know it but many live in some kind of denial, morbid dread, or perpetual procrastination.

Some say outright that they are in no hurry to get right with God because it may be a thousand years before Jesus returns. Don't be silly. He is going to come or call for you during your lifetime. For more than 50 years I have stood with families beside the empty, waiting graves of their loved ones ranging from pre-birth to 90 plus. Most somehow knew the event was coming but were surprised at the timing. It's a difficult time for those left behind. It is an awesome time for those who die in the Lord!

In case I get to say something at your funeral I thought I should give you a heads up on what I'd like to say.

First, I'll be sure everyone knows whose funeral it is. As best I can I will share a little of your own testimony including what others and I have observed.

Then, I hope to assure everyone present of three or four parts of unchangeable truth about death:

1) <u>You have an appointment with death</u>, but I don't know the date and time. God's Word says, *"...it is appointed unto men once to die, but after this the*

judgment:" I'll be sure to remind everyone that God did not make that death appointment, but we still have to keep it. I will assure people that Jesus came, died the first and second death, and faced judgment for us and ahead of us. The death appointment for the Believer is a breeze. You should know that those who are born only once must die twice, but those who are born twice must die only once.

2) I plan to say to everyone that <u>death is not the cessation of</u> <u>existence</u>. With God's help I will do my best to show your family and friends, from God's Word and human efforts through the years, that life does indeed continue after death. This earthly body of flesh and blood is temporary.

3) It is important that I say to your folks that <u>death as</u> <u>we know it is not the worst thing that can happen to</u> <u>someone</u>. I plan to say that the plight of existing without fellowship with God their Creator and Redeemer is the most serious plight of all. I'll probably tell them that is true before and after death. I imagine I'll quote Jesus, *Do not be afraid of those who kill the body, but cannot kill the soul. Rather, be afraid of the One who can destroy both soul and body in hell." – Matthew 10:28*

4) Finally I plan to let none of your folks get away without knowing that <u>Jesus Christ has won a decided</u> <u>victory over death</u>, and that victory is for everyone who surrenders their life to Jesus Christ before they die. I'll give them God's Word for this truth.

This information is morbid <u>*only*</u> for the unprepared.

Here's a thought. In case any of you are still alive, expect to hear someone say at my funeral what I would have said at yours.

Meanwhile, maybe you and I both will bypass the grave via our Lord's call to meet Him in the air!

Not To Choose Is To Choose

This thing of choosing puts an awesome responsibility on us. In fact, it is impossible not to choose. Not to choose is a choice to let someone else choose. Not to choose makes a vacuum. Somebody will fill it.

So, what am I saying? Your life is made up of choices. Every day is filled with choices. As a small child, many of your activities were chosen by someone else. As you matured, more and more of your decisions and activities have been your choice.

Sometime ago I heard someone say that we are only a choice away from defeat and destruction. That sounded so precarious, so fragile and risky! I took another look at it and thought to myself, we are only a choice away from victory, success, and life!!!

After mulling over that thought and trying to use it in writing something affirming to a friend, it began to jell. Here is the outcome:

The Measure of a Man

The measure of a man is made
By the choices of the man measured.
Each choice of that man is chosen
By the values of life that man chooses.

The values of life that man chooses
  Are made by that man's measure of his
  Maker.
So the span of that man from the womb to the sod
  Is measured by that man's measure of his
  God.
Then a measured man's choices by the values he
chooses
  Set the final score whether he wins or he
  loses.

- JSM 11/02

Having difficulty with some of your choices? Check your values!

Your values not steadily aligned? Who is your god? Just a god, or God! I read somewhere that a man's <u>loyalty</u> is directly related to his view of Christ's <u>ROYALTY</u>!

It's your choice! Do you choose to choose or do you choose not to choose and thereby choose to let circumstances, fate, or someone else choose?

Think about it!

You have just chosen!

Your Experience, or God's Appearance...

Or both?
Both! Read on..

The pendulum keeps swinging, _God's Appearance_ – true Biblical information, sound theology, understanding God at work; or _Your Experience_ -testimony, what's happening now, even seeing God to be more like you.

This is shaky ground. Too far in one direction can be right, biblically right, dead right. Too far in the other direction you can, in your thrills, lose your mooring and embark without chart or compass. That too can spell d-e-a-t-h, separation from intimacy with your Lord.

Your Experience can be centered in your need. God's Appearance is centered in His answer. You need both!

Without God's Word as anchor and the Holy Spirit as compass, your "experience" can become God's "ex-appearance."

When the predominant emphasis is on knowing about God, the hope is then that those who properly understand will decide to become followers of Christ and develop into mature Christians.

When people's primary point of receptivity is personal need and experience, then, after knowing God, it is essential to know more about Him and follow on to know Him better.

Hear me. Experience with all its feelings and thrills is awesome! But remember – <u>Your Experience</u> may have no deep roots apart from <u>God's Appearance</u>, His presence.

We are in an age dominated by experience. Advertising, events out there, and even church is saturated with experience mentality. The dominant question to children, even adult children is, "Was it fun?" Fun is also the first three letters of funeral.

Fun for fun's sake is empty. Fun as a result of what is right is great! Experience for experience sake is risky. Experiencing God's presence is not only awesome, it is redemptive, restorative, and sustaining!

Oswald Chambers once wrote, *"When we are in an unhealthy state...we always want thrills. In the physical domain this will lead to counterfeiting the Holy Ghost; in the emotional life it leads to inordinate affection and the destruction of morality; and in the spiritual domain if we insist on getting thrills...it will end in the destruction of spirituality."*

Your steady walk with the Lord is not dependent upon your Experience. It is nothing you initiate. When you Experience because of God's Appearance, your Experience is to be a response to God's Appearance!

Your Experience, or God's Appearance, or both? Both!

Tall Okra and High Worship

I didn't say "high church." This is about High Worship!
Some people down home used to say, and I think believe,
that a person's posture while planting okra determined how
tall the okra plants would be. They said for tall okra, stand
tall, straight up while dropping the seeds. For short plants
where short people could reach the okra pods easily, stoop
very low while dropping the seeds.

The whole idea put the gardener, by his posture, in control
of the okra growth and harvesting.

I learned later that the height of okra was determined by
the particular variety of seed, assuming the fertilizer, soil,
care, and weather are right. But the posture of the gardener?
Aren't some of the old notions interesting?

I got to thinking about all that okra stuff while considering worship. During worship a leader declared that anyone
not standing and not participating in some other physical
expression was not worshipping. One man said to his wife,
"Well, I guess we can no longer worship. We are not physically capable."

Across town and equally across other's expectations
some folks were dancing with joy and gratitude to God for
His forgiveness and awesome deliverance in their lives. They
were told that their disrespectful behavior was totally inappropriate and a gross hindrance to people trying to worship.

Worship, high worship. When is it? When is it not? How much does it have to do with my physical posture or my soul expression at the moment? Are my expressions my worship, or even the cause of my worship?

Sometimes when our children and grandchildren are home there are a lot of goings on all over the place at the same time. The little ones are all engrossed in one thing, and their parents are all remembering and sharing and laughing while the teens are in another world. For all they know, I am asleep on the recliner. What they don't know is that I'm basking with glee in their enjoyment. Furthermore, I get to hear some things that I probably would not hear if they had but known. We're a family - we are one.

In worship, corporate worship, I believe Father God embraces a variety of genuine worship from his children with a variety of expressions we all bring from our private worship, plus. The sum total is much greater than the combination of separate parts. Something exponential happens when we are gathered together in faith. That faith reaches God but also embraces the personal differences of fellow believers who are equally committed and obedient to God.

But back to "Tall Okra and High Worship." The key element for tall okra is the seed, not the demeanor of the gardener. The Bible says that the rains come, causing plants to bud and flourish and produce seed, "so is my word that goes out of my mouth."

High worship is not caused by the demeanor of the worshipper. The heart and security of high worship is the Seed, God's Word, always accompanied by Christ, the Living Word, and inspired by the Holy Spirit.

Look around. He who is the same yesterday, today, and forever, expresses Himself in ultra variety.

The oil of the Holy Spirit enables us to stretch without breaking. We can then include a variety of components of expression but ever cling to God's Word, the Seed, insuring real High Worship!

Drive-by Blessings,
or God's Residence?

Many years ago I went to preach at a certain church. The parking lot was full when I arrived. A man I knew drove up, let down his window, and spoke to me. His car was filled with his family. He asked me if I would pray for his 15 year old son who was diagnosed with terminal cancer.

I assured the father it was great to see him and we would pray for his son. In fact, I told him he and his family would have a great time of worship with us, and a message from God's Word would help prepare for the healing. He immediately told me he had other plans, didn't have time, and sped away. Later I learned of his son's funeral.

Drive-by blessings. They're still scarce.

Recently a lady from Huntsville saw one of my sons down at Cape Canaveral where they were both on TDY. She asked him if there was anything going on at the church here on Sunday nights. He told her about our healing service the first Sunday night of each month. She came, desperate for healing. She had a ringing in her ears that had been beyond medical help for a long time. After a message on Jesus question, "Do You Want To Be Well?" she immediately went to the altar for prayer.

Two or three people prayed for and with her. Some people went briefly for prayer and left. She stayed. She just continued in prayer and submitting to God as others prayed for her. She yielded. She was desperate.

After the benediction someone said, "Pastor, there's a testimony over here." I immediately took the mike and asked the people to listen up. She was flat on her back on the floor, radiant with joy. I put the mike to her mouth and she gave enthusiastic testimony that the ringing was gone and she was healed!

It is good not to be in too big of a hurry for God. He is looking for more than drive-bys. But read on.

People had begun their friendly interacting again when another lady tapped me on the shoulder. A health-care lady assisting one of our elderly members said, "Pastor, I'm not one for standing up and talking to a bunch of people, but I have been filled with hate for 13 years for the person who killed my son at that time. Tonight God has taken that hate away!" Again everyone was called to attention and erupted in celebration as they heard of her miracle!

It pays not to rush away. After Jesus' miracle of turning water into wine, the MC told the groom that people expect the best up front but they were getting the choice wine at the end.

It was on the last day of a great feast that Jesus declared the awesome promise of streams of living water.

Those who just go by only for an appearance and taste miss God's best. I read again the awesome provisions in Psalm 91 are to those who dwell in the secret place of the most High and <u>who abide</u> under the shadow of the Almighty. They are not drive-bys.

"They that wait upon the Lord shall renew their strength; they shall mount up with wings as eagles; they shall run, and not be weary; and they shall walk, and not faint." Isaiah 40:31 (KJV)

Praying Saying What God Says

M ost people who pray know that God already knows everything. He is omniscient. What I mean here is that we intentionally include in our prayers statements of God's actions and promises in the past, information that we know God already says.

In the Spring of 1956, I was called to the Jefferson-Hillman Hospital (now UAB) to pray for a high profile businessman in Birmingham, who, as I recall, was injured in a fall. During that visit, as so often occurs, I felt that I got more than I gave. Here's the story he shared with me.

During World War II, he was a flight instructor and the hill country of north Alabama was part of the terrain where his student pilots trained. One day he and a student pilot were flying in a certain area when the student lost control in a rugged ravine. They crashed. Neither was seriously injured, but the incident came under thorough investigation. Among the digging questions, the investigator asked the pilot if he noticed any kind of different behavior or activities of the instructor at the time of the crash. The pilot responded with a yes, that the instructor crossed his fingers. The investigator turned to him for an explanation.

He told the investigator that before going on the flight he had prayed earnestly to God for direction and protection. He said he then told God that in case of an emergency where he could not stop and pray, that he would cross his fingers and that was the sign language repeating the prayer he had earnestly prayed earlier. In that crisis he had crossed his fingers. That too, is saying what God says. In fact, that is real intensely compressed prayer, instantly re-praying what the pray-er and God was already saying and have agreed upon.

In the Bible some of the prayers were like a review of history – His story in their lives and the lives of their people. God was often addressed as the "God of Abraham, Isaac, and Jacob." Sometimes God's activities in the lives of those men were verbalized in the prayer.

You see, prayer is not just a "want list" we give to God. It is a way of hanging out with God for awhile and talking over things of interest to both of you, God and you. "God-ship" is what I'm talking about. Fellowship is two or more fellows interacting together. "Godship" must be one or more people having some time and interaction with God.

Anyhow, God knows what we have need of even before we ask. Much of prayer is for the purpose of getting in sync with God so we can know His heart better and thereby make our petitions according to His will. That may be what we mean by "praying through."

One way of praying, saying what God says, is to "prayer-a-phrase." That is a word I believe the Lord gave me several years ago to describe praying the Scripture. Prayer-a-phrasing is taking a portion of Scripture, what God is saying, and praying it back to God. You can get some great help in the Christian classic, PRAYING THE SCRIPTURES, by Judson Cornwall.

The more you enter into God-talk and God-walk, the more you enter into God's will and God's way. Then prayer results are a given. God has directed us to pray, and prayer is more than just a field exercise in preparation for the real thing. Prayer **is** the real thing!

Don't You Sell Your Home!!!

Your house? Maybe. Your HOME? Never!
Some have even traded their home for a house, a cheap house at that. When they do they wind up paying an awful price for a cheap piece of merchandise.

I once knew a man who had a house and a family but didn't have a home. To get to his house was not easy. He lived in a small unkempt house by the side of an unmarked path from a larger trail, through a weed field. The larger trail branched off the end of a two-rut, less-than-a-road, from a county road off the main dirt road at the edge of our community.

Jack could not read or write but he was a hard worker. He didn't own a car so he walked to work. Work place, and place of origin, was in town about eight miles away. He dug graves with pick and shovel. Jack came to church. His blue bib overalls looked so fresh and clean.

I remember the night Jack got saved. A guest preacher, thought to be uncultured and incompetent by many, communicated the need for salvation and the saving grace of Jesus. Jack heard and obeyed. There was a major turn-around in his life. That is called repentance.

A couple of behaviors in Jack's life gave evidence to the community that a home began occupying and operating from his house. Of course, he became a worshipper, but it takes more than that to build a home.

It was a Saturday morning. From my car window I saw a man and a little boy walking on their way home from fishing. Each had a fishing pole across his shoulder and a big grin on his face. The boy had a string of fish in his hand. A father and son were bonding. Jack and David, without knowing it, were announcing to all who passed by, that a home was emerging and occupying that house over by that path through the field.

You can have a house without a home. You can also have a home without a house. It is great when you can have both.

Don't you sell your home!!! There is no price high enough!

For years I have been bothered by "Homes for Sale" in the newspaper. Even though I know what they mean it still bothers me.

No house, good or bad, can ever replace a home – a good stable one.

Jesus said, *"My peace I give unto you."* He makes the peace He gives. In fact, He is our peace.

The Bible says, *"Accept one another as Christ accepted you."*

The proving ground for a home may be all the *"one anothers"* in the Bible. The best place to first practice the "Fruit of the Spirit" is in your home.

Here are some Bible "one another" ingredients for your home:

Be devoted to one another	*Give preference to one another*
Love one another	*Admonish one another*
Pray for one another	*Care for one another*
Serve one another	*Be kind to one another*
Do not lie to one another	*Forgive one another*
Comfort one another	*Encourage one another*

70

A house alone won't do it. It takes a home in the house, and it takes the Creator of the home living in the family in the house to make it function! Those same ingredients for a home are essential in each one's personal life. That's how they enter the home. You can start an epidemic in your house and cause it to become a home.

Don't you sell your home! Your house? Maybe. Your home? Never!

About Marriage, Cook'n, and Kiss'n

I'm writing this on the night of our 50th Wedding Anniversary in a state of disbelief. Can this really be? 50?

Let me talk a little about 50, and marriage, and life, and a little that younger guessers apparently don't yet know.

On May 1, 1960, a "very old couple," I thought, the Rev. and Mrs. Allie Dantzler, celebrated their 50th. Their family and friends had a big celebration. Janelle and I couldn't go because she was up at the hospital having a baby and thought I should stay around. A few days later I went over to visit the Dantzlers and grinned when I read a plaque on the wall that one of the youngsters had given them. I read it with mixed emotions: "Kiss'n Don't Last, but Cook'n Do." While I was grinning, I was soberly pondering.

It didn't bother me long though because 50 years would never arrive anyway. But it has and I have finally reached the point in life that I can talk about that plaque. It is only about 25% true. Cooking doesn't just last, it gets better too! That's all that is true.

A young lady, with a real quest for an answer, asked me, "How can somebody be married for 50 years?" My quick and simple answer was, "Well, get married, then stay married and pretty soon it will happen." Then I mentioned just a tidbit of what I want to share with you now.

When I mentioned in an almost flippant way that Janelle and I were going to a "Pre-50th Prep," it was truer than I realized. *Intimate Life Ministries* led a two-day retreat that we attended. Nobody "pulled a rabbit out of a hat" and startled us with any magic. What we did do was review the ingredients of a good, well maybe great relationship that finds it's most complete portrayal in marriage.

The more these ingredients are present and the better they are developed, a continual process, the quicker the big 5-0 will come. The way to be sure your marriage lasts a looonnnggg time without reaching 50 is to avoid, or at least not develop these ingredients.

Just as sure as you have need of air, water, food, and sleep you have other needs. In addition to your spiritual needs from God like love, forgiveness, peace, and more, you have certain relational needs. We are not created, redeemed, or married to be alone. Dr. David Ferguson taught at the two-day retreat that "we have a God-given need to receive and to give these elemental ingredients:

Appreciation	Affection	Attention
Acceptance	Approval (Blessing)	Comfort
Encouragement	Respect	Support
Security (Peace)"		

I would add Communication to that list. Come to think of it those words constitute good communication. Remember the elderly couple sitting on the front porch in their rocking chairs quietly staring at the setting sun? Finally Henry spoke. He said, "You know Lizzy, sometimes I get to thinking of how much I love you and it takes all I can do to keep from telling you."

Intentional, deliberate communication is vital!

Looking back now on those elemental ingredients, Janelle and I, without identifying them at the time have tried to practice them and we still have them in development. We both are benefiting. In marriage "kiss'n" is a long lasting word, spelled approvalaffectionattentionacceptancecomfortencouragementrespectsupportsecurity and pronounced "communication."

Yeah, kiss'n lasts, but it takes two, giving and receiving!

Without all these ingredients, it could just be a fake — just lip-synching!

Help Me, Lord, To Hate!

I want to be more and more God-like. My God who is love also hates. In order to love like God loves I need to hate what He hates.

Help me, Lord, to hate what You hate like You hate it. Maybe I should first love what/whom You love the way You love. I believe I'm hearing You as I write, Lord.

Oh yes, I'm to love all people but hate all wrong, all sin.

You said in Your Word for me to "hate evil and love good." Then why don't You fix in me a well-defined identification of all evil and set my thermometer on "hate?" Then please adjust my love gage to be unaffected by that which I am to hate, and set it automatically on "good." I think I'd like that.

Oh, You didn't create or redeem me to be a robot? Then, please, Lord, help me to hate properly.

Okay, I'm reading it right here what You have already sent me, *"...six things the Lord hates, seven that are detestable to him: haughty eyes, a lying tongue, hands that shed innocent blood, a heart that devises wicked schemes, feet that are quick to rush into evil, a false witness who pours out lies and a man who stirs up dissension among brothers.."* Prov. 6:16-19.

But Lord, I thought, in fact, at the top of my list were cussing, smoking, doing drugs, stealing, child abuse, and maybe spouse mistreatment. Oh, those come from deeper roots? The real problem is spiritual? Between You and me?

Then, Lord, did You inspire C. S. Lewis to pen these words a long time ago?

"The sins of the flesh are bad, but they are the least bad of all sins. All the worst sins are spiritual: the pleasure of putting other people in the wrong, of bossing and patronizing and backbiting; the pleasures of power, of hatred. For there are two things inside me, competing with the human self, which I must try to become. They are the Animal self, and the Diabolical self. The Diabolical self is worse."
– (Mere Christianity by C.S. Lewis)

Then Lord, I take it that You will lead, but I am responsible for following you? I'm beginning to hear You more clearly. I am to love You and Your ways, and concurrently hate the devil and his ways. I think I'm hearing that my greater love for You and Your ways will be what will help me to properly hate what You hate the way You hate it.

Is it really true that "sin is red-handed mutiny against you," Lord?

I believe I'm getting it Lord. I recall that You came to destroy the works of the devil. You refused to shirk, went head-on, and died in battle to deal with the devil and all evil. Yet I know now that You willingly laid Your life down for me and rose again to see that Your will can be executed in my life. You must have had an incalculable hatred for evil!

I take it that Your will is for me to be like You in love and hate. In Your love I submit to line up with You.

Oh, I can't do it by myself? Wow, You sent Your Holy Spirit to live in me bringing all Your power and sufficiency?

Yes, yes, Lord! I surrender! You said when I submit to You that I can resist the devil and he will flee. Here I am. Have it Your way!

Lord, I prayed for You to help me to hate! You are doing it again, giving more than I asked! As my love for You and Your ways exceeds my desires for this world then I can properly hate what You hate as you hate it. Thank You, Lord!"

Mourning? Now Find Your Morning!

Mourning is a verb, something you do, dealing with death.

Morning is a noun, a daily gift, announcing life!

Mourning is expressing deep sorrow, laden with sadness, of what was but cannot naturally be re-gained.

Morning is a new day, a new beginning. When morning begins it is still dark. It cannot be recognized by any of your five senses. At 12:01 a.m. it is actually morning but you have to accept it by sheer faith in the clock. Later daylight comes. You can then recognize morning by sight. With the sound of birds and other creatures, your hearing tells you it is morning.

Morning abounds with new life and fresh hope.

Life is filled with mourning and mornings. Losses, disappointments, deaths, and failures keep mourning in the present tense for many people. As sure as there was a resurrection morning after Jesus' death and the disciples' mourning, there is morning awaiting you! Find it!

Everybody knows there is mourning after the death of a loved one, and after your favorite football team is defeated by an underdog. But mourning lurks even closer.

Some people cannot enjoy family gatherings for mourning over non-recoverable events and people of some yesteryear. Some miss untold celebrations due to former celebrations that cannot be replicated. They mourn without hope of a morn. It's just too much!

In church anniversaries and family reunions, years of life are celebrated. In order to celebrate, we remember many great events and people of the past. Those memories are likely to tap some moments of mourning. Some of us will recall certain disappointments. Sorrow is likely to accompany those memories. Then some recall times of absolute grandeur! We may mourn that those people did not become fixed at that same age, and those events weren't kept in perpetual present tense for us.

Do you remember a child telling a joke and everyone laughing? In his jubilation he repeated it. Then after about the seventh time his little story was not nearly so funny. The listeners had rather hear a new story.

Have you learned that God in His creativity has new stories in the making for us? Have you learned that our God has an inexhaustible supply of mornings filled with ideas and resources and miracle events?

Some of us remember, recall, and tell again and again great stories of God at work in and among us! We celebrate! Sure, it is a "memory lane" but with those memories let us praise God, thank God and one another, and celebrate hilariously. Sometimes mourning, followed by "used to be's" gets scrambled in all that.

But listen! God has mornings, new mornings! From where some are, it is still pitch dark! But trust what you are hearing from the bow of this "old ship." It is morning!

It is time to transition from mourning to morning!

Turn, re-plant, and prepare for the greatest harvest yet in your personal life, the corporate life of your church, and the Body of Christ across the world!

The Bible says that God has turned my mourning into dancing.

"Restore our fortunes, Lord, as streams renew the desert. Those who plant in tears will harvest with shouts of joy. They weep as they go to plant the seed, but sing as they return with the harvest." - Ps. 126:4-6 (NLT)

How To Back Up Forward

It can be done. It is done.

Most of us back up forward each morning when we back out of the driveway to go to work. Though it is backing up it is forward in purpose. But that is not what I'm talking about here.

Some who read this may even remember driving a Model T Ford. Sometimes they found the car incapable of going straight forward up a long steep hill. They would turn the car around and back up the hill with no problem. They backed up forward.

One of my brothers-in-law told me that when he was young his father owned a car and would allow him to use it on a date or something, but with limited miles. He said when he exceeded the mileage he would back up for miles to reduce the odometer reading. That is one kind of backing up forward, but not what I have in mind.

How to back up forward?

The older I get the more I seem to back up forward. I am sure you do too. Let's look at it a little. Some awesome pictures from the past flash onto our memory screens.

All of this is to remind us of God's faithfulness in the past while we recall that *He is the same yesterday, today and forever.* That's backing up forward.

We back up forward when we confess our sins of the past, repent, and turn to God in obedience to Him. That's when we back up to deal with the un-dealt-with, backing up but really a forward action.

How to back up forward?

Someone told me that the backing up forward of the old automobiles had something to do with the *transmission*, a proper shifting of gears or something.

For us to back up forward has something to do with *transition*. Our back up forward includes memories of God at work in recent events, people, and places, but also the vast array of God at work in Bible times until now!

We need the assurance of all God's yesterdays as fodder for our faith today and tomorrow. But listen. We've crossed that Red Sea, fed on that manna, circled that mountain! Some of us have tasted the milk, and honey and grapes of the Promised Land still ahead! We, as people of faith, are ready to back up forward right into God's next level of His calling for us!

It was a major *transition* for those who stepped out in obedience and paved the way for you. Many have made certain *transitions* to bring all of us to where we are. Now, *let us look unto Jesus the author and finisher of our faith…"*

We face and follow *the Father of lights, with whom is neither variableness, or shadow of turning.* Going with God is never backward. This is a consternation to those who have only a "worm's eye view" of life. They limit their thinking to straight-line increments of cubicle thoughts.

Our God is not only our great example and leader going before us. He is also our rear guard. So, in Him we may back up forward!

May each of us believe God for a vision of *transition* into God's fresh calling!

This vision of *transition* must go beyond a view of yesterday. May it vibrate with a forward sound of victory!

Finding Thread for Your Prayers

Small prayers and infrequent praying may be due to the pray-er's shortage of thread. As you know, meaningful and effective prayers are multifaceted. Each prayer is more like a fabric with many threads and hues of colors. Some are short, bleak, and meaningless, if a prayer at all.

Here's a short 19 second prayer that just about sums up the "prayer life" of some: *"God, give me enough money to make it this month. I need money for my house payment, food, and utilities. Heal Mama and make my wife content. Get my children out of trouble, and bless all for whom it is my duty to pray. Amen."* You may be able to get it down to 15 seconds. But, really, dear ones, that is not praying. That's more like a husband saying to his wife, "Woman, you know I love you. I told you the day we were married. Now get that breakfast ready! I've got to go!"

God loves you and likes to have time with you. In fact, He likes you.

Praying is not just talking to God. Praying is talking with God. You know as well as I, that praying includes praise, thanksgiving, confessions, repentance, requests, promises, commitments of giving as well as asking, and all that. But that is not the thread I'm talking about here. Are you ready?

The thread that interlaces the structure, and weaves the fabric of your prayers, comes right from your own life.

What you've been thinking, reading, doing, talking about, and observing in others is the fiber that should thread your prayers.

Now, some of that thread will move into the praise and thanksgiving. Some must be woven into the confession and repentance. All should call for hearing in your spirit what the Holy Spirit is saying to you in response.

You see, prayer is communing with God. It is speaking and listening to God. The element that shortens prayers is the reluctance to go into certain areas. Talk with God about all the matters going on in your life. Include the many threads. You will be amazed at the amount of prayer there is to pray, the fulfillment that occurs, and how much shorter longer prayers seem.

This is a call to thread your prayer with more than artificial recitations and pious platitudes to please others. That is difficult, boring and meaningless. You know something about prayer structure, so get on with threading your prayer with your life and be blessed with the fabric!

"Infospiration"
Is The Right Word

Don't look for it in the dictionary. It's not there yet. Sometimes people get all inspired only to find their new inspiration was based on incorrect information. The letdown can be devastating.

Sometimes people endure meticulous and endless information, even accurate information, but they just can't get motivated to do anything about it. It just remains flat and lifeless.

Then there are those who get all inspired with valid, genuine, information that is pulsating with life. Wow! But what do you call it? How about *"infospiration!"* That means inspiration that is based upon genuine information. Get all you can! Can all you get!

Now, how does all this pan out?

It may be the difference between hope and *hope*, or hope and hype. Mere human hope and vibrant Christian *hope* are different. One is wistful thinking. The other is confident assurance.

Mere inspiration may connect, or it may be only a roulette chance and leave you with a popped bubble. But *"infospiration?"* It is substantive!

As a child, I often experienced high inspiration just prior to Christmas. I built my hopes on incorrect information. Once I learned that my inspiration was based on misinformation, I readjusted my expectations. From then on, I have experienced great *"infospiration"* every Christmas.

My early Christian life went "be-bop-a-lu-la" for a while. I was trying to build my life on my initial jubilance, someone else's testimony, and/or one or two out-of-context Scriptures. I must admit that slight vestiges of that hyped inspiration still crop up from time to time.

I'm finding *"infospiration"* a major prevention and cure for those thin times.

For instance, I once thought Jesus had one post-baptism rendezvous with temptation and that was it. I expected the same. Then I learned that Jesus' big victory in the Wilderness Temptation was not a once-and-for-all event. He was dogged by the devil all the way to Calvary, tempted in all things like we are, yet without sin. *"Infospiration"* is the word.

I somehow got the idea that I was to pray for people to be saved and they would get saved whether or not they wanted to be.

I once thought that I should just go around indiscriminately praying for anyone who is sick and expect them to be healed. Some time ago I began, and am still, learning God's will to heal the whole person – spirit, soul, and body – not just the body. Disappointments and confusion drove me to more of the reality, genuine information, in Christ and all God's Word. It is amazing how healing flows into our bodies when the spiritual roots of bitterness, hatred, unforgiveness, resentment, self-rejection, and other junk are removed from our lives by faith in the shed blood of Jesus on Calvary. *"By His stripes we are healed."*

I'm talking about *"infospiration,"* not just short-term inspiration that may, or may not connect with and give on-going benefit.

"Infospiration" has to do with, and is vitally connected with Jesus' directive for us to know and teach others *"to observe all the things that He has commanded us."* With that directive He has promised to be with us always, even to the end of the age! All this is included in **discipleship** where infospiration is resident!

Crucifix or Crucified/Risen: Re-Connect

E aster is the season when we think more about Christ's Passion, the Cross, and His Resurrection! And we should!

But I'm bothered. There seems to be a disproportionate absence of our Lord's core redemptive mission in much of what I'm hearing these days. Yes, I'm hearing this preacher's voice also.

Is our seasonal Christianity contributing to the insipid impact the church is having on the world today?

All this is riveting my soul with one hard question: Am I really crucified and risen with Christ, or am I counting on just a fix, a mere crucifix.

A crucifix is a cross with the figure of someone's idea of Jesus Christ on it. To some it is only a sentimental good luck charm. Of course, it is religious. I don't have a crucifix, but I do have several crosses as pins, book marks, a necklace, etc. These must never be a substitute for my identification on the Cross, by faith, with Jesus Christ, and risen with Him in newness of life.

The Apostle Paul said, *"I have been crucified with Christ and I no longer live, but Christ lives in me. The life I live in*

*the body, I live by faith in the Son of God, who loved me and
gave himself for me." Gal. 2:20*

I am bothered that many may be counting on a mere <u>fix</u>
with the symbols of the Christian faith without ever personally experiencing the vital relationship with Jesus Christ.

The mere crucifix may be no more than an effort to identify with the general Christian idea, just a detached item
stretching to include the owner.

To be crucified with Christ is a whole different dimen-
sion. It is an act of faith whereby you identify with Christ
and His death to the point of mortifying all sinful motives
and acts of the flesh. You can't do it alone, but God in His
grace has given His Holy Spirit to enable you. The choice is
still yours to surrender or not surrender to Him. It is a "sell
out" to Jesus Christ whereby your sinful nature is totally
surrendered and His risen life has liberty of expression. A
mere <u>fix</u>, even a cruci<u>fix</u>, will never do that. A surrendered,
submitted relationship will.

God is calling us to be more than itinerant fruit pickers
of selected blessings. He desires fellowship with us that we
may be partakers of His Holiness with all His grace and
power at work within us in our daily lives.

Please go beyond a tradition, a name, a symbol, a memory,
an idea…a cruci<u>fix</u>. Let God reveal to you the gain, then you
can deal with any pain. Let Him show you the crown, then
you can bear the cross all the way to crucifying the sinful
flesh. There you find breakthrough into the high provisions
of your life crucified with Christ and vibrant in His risen
life!

The Great Debate: Jesus Aloof?

This debate may be the issue that divides real Christianity from some ancient religion often portrayed as "christianity" - is, or is not, Jesus aloof?

I'll forever remember Janelle's and my first visit to Israel. To actually see and put my feet on the land of the Bible was beyond my fondest imaginations.

My body was moving faster than my mind. We arrived in Tel Aviv, and were bussed straight to Jerusalem late that first night. The next morning we were up and out early. The weather was cloudy, and drizzling. Within minutes we walked over some apparent ruins and right into the temple area of old Jerusalem. I was struggling to get out of the cocoon of my daze. Immediately an old, unshaven, and somewhat unkempt man approached us asking for money. Temple tax or something he called it. In my cocoon I briefly thought I had walked back into Bible days and that man was one of the characters I ought to recognize. Some of us quickly gave.

I was caught in the great debate: Is Jesus Christ and my faith in Him aloof, archaic? Could it be that HE is relevant NOW for me?

My mind began catching up that day for that and subsequent trips into Bible lands.

Thankfully I broke out of that "daze" cocoon!

I continued, however, to wrestle with the time-era of my faith. It's fairly easy to accept and believe in someone and/or some information as long as it remains dormant in the past. It's easy but not very interesting.

I'm talking about a faith that either is or is not. If my faith is aloof, then Jesus Christ is aloof. He is basically stuck in that past time-era, and not even freed from that crowd and their garb, their customs, and the ruins of old Jerusalem.

The Christ of "archaic christianity" can remain aloof. Such a person, stuck in a past era, where I am not, has no fellowship with me, offers no help to me, and requires nothing of me. Could that be a kind of cocoon religion? Aloof christianity?

If there really was a cross and death of Jesus Christ, and if He really did go through the grave into an eternal resurrection, then our Christ is not aloof!

If Jesus Christ is not aloof, then followers of Jesus Christ, Christians, can no longer be aloof! I've been inside His grave. It is empty!

The truth is, historically He did live, die and live again then. Through faith Christ really does live now. Alive Christians serving the living Christ have fellowship with Him, and we can share in His Life, receive help from Him, and are accountable to Him!

He is more than Lord of the ruins of long ago. He offers to be Lord of our ruins, and turn them into righteousness! He is not aloof!

You are invited to draw near to Him and he will draw near to you!

The great debate may still be raging for some, but rest assured Jesus Christ is not aloof! He is alive, He is close and He cares.

My Defenseless Body Needs Help

S trange things happen on the way to heaven and other places. This morning I woke up early and confirmed that I was alive. Then I sort of dozed off, but some really awakening thoughts began running through my mind. I am days away from brain surgery.

I imagined what would be happening if I had not awakened. I knew that somebody would have to dispose of my body. In case nobody would have sped up the "ashes to ashes, dust to dust" thing then I imagined the other possibility. Somebody probably would wash my face and neck, clean my fingernails, and comb my hair. Then they'd dress my body in that dark suit I bought a couple of years ago.

I became really concerned about what expression they'd put on my face. I like to have some say-so in that. Then they would put out my defenseless body on a cooling board, now called a casket, so viewers could come by and look.

I imagined curious people making verbal comments with a silent conjunction, like "I heard Joel preach a pretty good sermon one time," then silently thinking, "however…" or "but…" or "albeit…" and swallow the rest without going vocal. I actually got tickled.

Then I was from somewhere looking at my defenseless body and all the goings-on around it, and thought to myself,

"My defenseless body needs help now, not just after I leave it!"

I think you know what I'm talking about. My body doesn't get much say-so in what it does or where it goes. Sometimes it puts up a fuss and gets its way, but that is just sometimes. It has to eat what I put in its mouth. It gets rest when I allow it, and keeps going when I demand it. My body is also subject to many factors — weaknesses, strengths, looks, and more — that my ancestors contributed. Defenseless again, but I think I have a responsibility to deal with those factors in every way possible on behalf of my body.

The defenseless element that concerns me most, however, is right here in the now. When I move out of my body others will take over, but with fewer options than I have now.

Right now these many options really put a lot of responsibility on my soul—mind, emotions, and will—to make the right choices. Are the choices I make enslaving my body or freeing it? Is my body free to live within the boundaries of maximum health, strength, productivity, and longevity? Does my defenseless body find security and hope within the guidelines I give and enforce? Or, is it a slave?

My defenseless body needs all the help it can get!

Personally I am not concerned with what "they" do to or with my defenseless body when I leave it. I will be getting a new one.

Right now I am reminded that this body in which I live is not really mine to do with as I please. It is bought with a price. It belongs to the One who designed and created it. I am to care for this body and please God with it. It is not just where I live. It is the dwelling place of the Holy Spirit also, my Bible says.

I'm wide awake now! My defenseless body needs help, and I'm the first responder! Who's helping your body?!

The Tale of Two Skulls

This tale is true. Written in late April, 2008.

We have unintentionally discovered an enemy alien prowling in my skull. He was found while we were looking for another suspected villain.

This is amazing! You know how sometimes they show on TV the picture of an intruder, caught by security cameras, in a place of business? Well, that's sort of what happened.

We not only have his picture, we know his name. He is Hemangioblastoma Tumor (H. T.). I told you he is an alien. He is operating in the cerebellum area of my skull. As best we can tell he is unarmed, benign, but can still cause a bunch of damage if not dealt with soon.

Several of God's deputies, physicians, have been carefully surrounding my skull and planning the best attack to remove H. T. This week the health squad has searched the area as far out as my chest, abdomen, and pelvic areas and found no other aliens giving back-up or assistance to H. T. in any way.

I think we're ready for the move to take H. T. out without a fight. Sometimes the "High Sheriff" Himself does sort of an "Andy Griffith" resolution and let's his deputies think they've done it all. Most of the time it is a total team effort.

What you have just read is not an air-tight medical report, but it is close.

Early Thursday morning after learning the particulars of name, location, unarmed status, and options, I was up early. While walking to the kitchen I heard this all inside me, "The Great Physician has been to *'the place of the skull'* and already won the greatest victory ever! He is now in the place of this skull." *(Read Matthew 27:33)*

I can live with that!

With all the MRIs, ex-rays, stress tests, lab work, and other things I can't remember or pronounce I probably have the best health report ever except for H.T. doing what he can bring harm.

I am so grateful! I give thanks to God, the medical team, and to all who have prayed for me!

"The place of the skull" is Golgotha, Calvary! That is where Jesus Christ *"was wounded for our transgressions... and by His stripes we are healed."*

"Every good and perfect gift comes from God" no matter who delivers it. *"Faith without works is dead."* For more than 40 years my stance has been, when I'm sick, to pray that God will heal me and then do everything I can to get well. I am convinced it is the Bible way. It works.

Most of the battles in the skull are not in the organic brain but in the mind. I believe God, and purpose to behave my belief to live in the total victory Christ won then at *"the place of the skull."*

I want more than the arrest and eviction of H. T. from my skull. I want the greater miracle, the resident occupancy of the mind of Christ functioning under the rule of the Holy Spirit!

That's the true tale of two skulls! It worked! It works!

Faith is Fabric, Not a Thread

A thread is only a fragment of a fabric. It may be beautiful. It may be ugly. It finds its real value when woven into the fabric.

Thoughts, ideas, and even beliefs reflect a variety of hues, some in conflict when alone, but in beauty when properly woven together. A designer can weave them into one beautiful (or obnoxious) fabric.

Christian faith is more than just a thread or a ball of threads. Some I've seen look more like a tangled wad of yarn. "Yarn" has more than one meaning, you know.

A thread, or even many disconnected threads, never has the strength of a fabric properly woven, connecting those same threads.

Faith is fabric, not just a thread!

Faith is more than a fabric. Faith is fabric. A faith is pretty exclusive. Even Christian faith is exclusive, but the Christian faith is fabric. It excludes competitive and conflicting beliefs, but the Christian faith is also inclusive. It includes the vast variety of threads that constitute the Christian faith.

A fabric is "in" today, but gone tomorrow. When I was a "card carrying" cloth cutter more than 50 years ago we cut fabrics with designs found now only in somebody's stuffy closet or attic. They're out.

Fabric is still "in" and will be. Some people seem to wear less and less of it, but it is still in.

Here is what got me onto this: The other morning when the nurse set the schedule for my possible surgery, she said I am to check into the hospital May 7, at 9 a.m. and the surgery is to be May 8, at 9 a.m. I immediately remembered a couple of other "nine o'clock in the mornings" and replied without comment, "I can go along with nine o'clock in the morning."

It was nine o'clock in the morning when Jesus went to the cross for me. The Holy Spirit was poured out at the third hour, 9 a.m., on the Day of Pentecost as recorded in Acts 2. So I thought to myself that will be extra significant for me.

Then I remembered that God is omni-present. Faith is not a fabric. Faith is fabric, not a thread.

Real Christian faith is to be perpetual as the One in whom we place our faith is perpetual.

Some of the threads, often entangled and called faith, are certain places, dates, times, issues, environment, circumstances, names, events, even political parties, and more.

Our God is the God who meets us on high days and holy days, but also on any other day when we call on Him. God is. I have experienced the God in whom I have my faith on Golgotha late at night and in the empty tomb at sunrise. My faith has been quickened with shepherds on the Judean hillside under the star speckled night canopy, and on the Sea of Galilee at midday. Christmas, Easter, Ascension Day, the Day of Pentecost, and every Lord's Day are meaningful times for me. The last Monday night of every March, my new birth birthday, is always significant.

Those and myriads of others are threads of various hues. Here are some more – grace, justice, mercy, forgiveness, healing, suffering, provisions, security, accountability, holiness, and, and, and…. These are threads when not woven into the fabric can become threadbare.

I am contending for fabric faith, not just a thread of faith. Any day, any time, any where!

Any takers?

Seeing God in the Inapt

The two areas people find it most difficult to see God at work are in the usual and the unusual, the apt and the inapt.

The apt are the usual, most expected, norm times. Those are the times and the events determined by the observer to be most suited, fitting, and appropriate.

The inapt are the unusual, least expectant, and abnormal times and events determined by the observer to be most unsuitable, unfitting, and inappropriate.

I received a call from a friend several states away. She is a very dedicated Christian with a lot of perception regarding the things of God. She wanted my honest, candid, and outright opinion about a widely publicized revival somewhere. I don't like questions like that. What does my opinion have to do with it anyhow?

I immediately remembered and shared with her about a local healing mission, sponsored by the Order of Saint Luke the Physician, we were having many years ago. John Parke from up in New England was our guest minister. During a question and answer session someone asked Parke what he thought about a certain radio preacher and what that preacher said about something. Parke replied, "I cannot speak about another minister and his ministry. However, I will be happy to share with you my understanding about a particular issue or subject." What grace!

You see, many people accept what God is doing only if it is in their personal norm. Their norm is based upon their experience and sometimes on their understanding of the Bible, and what they have seen and been told. I've wrestled with all that myself. Yet as I accumulate a growing history of God at work outside the ordinary in my life I am reminded more and more that he is operating outside and beyond my brain. I thought having my skull opened in brain surgery would help, but they closed it back up.

There are other people who seem to recognize God at work only when He is in the realm of the inapt. It just has to be God when it is in the unexpected, out of the ordinary! Some of those people find it difficult to see God in his ongoing operations of the universe, a song they have heard more than three times, the reading of God's word they may have heard before, and the established disciplines of the Christian Life.

I believe God wants us to recognize Him both in the usual and the unusual. We make a major step forward when we can turn loose control enough to just let God be God without having to vote or having to pass our opinion on what He is doing.

Many years ago I heard myself praying in the Spirit. I am sure it was in English, but it was also in the Spirit. I had an immediate prayer stoppage and lingered absorbing what had been prayed.

"Father God please help me not to misunderstand what I don't yet understand!"

Please join me in experiencing God in both the inapt and the apt! Sometimes in trying to fence God in, we may fence Him out! He is all over the place! With God's help, let's see Him at work in the apt and the inapt!

Blessed And Bothered
Go Together

I've been watching and reading a variety of portrayals of "churchianity" afloat these days. I am blessed and I am bothered.

Come to think of it blessings and botherings seem to have a way of hanging out together.

All this started surfacing sometime ago when various friends in different cities would share with me their search for a church in their new locale. I kept hearing, "We really like the music, but...." The preaching is great, but...." Their location is so close by, but..." The people are so friendly, but...."

So? That's life!

Everything that bothers me is not wrong, it's just different from what I'm used to. Janelle and I have been married for more than 50 years. We had a great wedding in Winston-Salem and a delightful few days' drive through the mountains to Birmingham where we would be living.

What a surprise I was in for! We went together to the supermarket to buy our first supply of kitchen stuff. I couldn't believe what I saw her do. She actually pulled from the shelf and put into the cart a can of Calumet baking powder! I immediately questioned her. I thought everybody cooked with Clabber Girl baking powder. Mama did. I was so bothered, but decided to deal with it. The blessing of those Calumet biscuits have far exceeded the bother!

Then there was this thing of music. I kept my bother quiet. Even then I had sense enough to know Janelle knew far more about music and worship than I ever would. I preferred songs about me – "I'll Fly Away," and "In a Land Where We'll Never Grow Old." She preferred for worship, songs about our Lord – "All Hail The Power of Jesus Name," and "Great Is Thy Faithfulness."

I needed to be bothered.

I needed to stretch or change or both.

Here is another. Aren't children a great blessing!? But they can also be a bother. The blessing and the bother go together!

Every week "church" is a blessing and a bother. I live with both. I re-live the whole worship every week – the music, singing, praying, preaching, responding in invitation, the length of time.....

The blessing always excels the bother. The two worst parts of that brain surgery I had were missing the worship with my church family and that bone-pounding headache. Missing worship may have been the worst.

I like to preach and I like to hear preaching. The preaching that bothers me more than any, is mine. But I'm not quitting to avoid being bothered. Some bother is conviction calling me to change. Some is observation calling me to improve. I'm blessed and bothered.

Worship is more like a kitchen where I go to feed than a laboratory where I go to analyze. I'm committed to bother forward into greater riches of God's blessings!

But That Was Not Meditating!

Out-right praying is what it was! In fact, it was closet-praying on a Georgia hillside.

Meditation is great but some prayer cannot be meditated. Here is one I vividly remembered about 4 o'clock this morning. It surfaced as I was being rewarded anew by a closet-prayer answered years ago.

I was awakened with a pressing message, I believe, from the Lord, "Your meditations are great, but your voiced praying is low in proportion." Then in a flash I saw and am living again that closet-prayer with my Lord's open reward more than 50 years ago.

It was November, 1956. I was a sophomore at Emmanuel College. We were into final exams for fall quarter. Everyone else was registering for the winter quarter. It suddenly dawned on me that I too was to register but I couldn't. I had no money.

My freshman year with a small scholarship at Birmingham Southern, free room and board at my sister's, and a weekly salary of $15 from Coalburg where I "pastored" were all past. There I stood staring reality in the face.

Quiet meditation was not cutting it, so I shifted into desperation praying. It was mid-afternoon. I needed space, yet I needed to be alone, closet-space. I went past the old cemetery on the edge of the campus and followed a little dirt road up a long hill. At the top I walked a distance to my right. Underneath some golden-leafed hickories, I knelt by a large apparent limestone boulder. At that time it still took about 200 acres for me to have total freedom in prayer. I felt I had a safe distance from others.

I don't remember all that I prayed. I do remember I prayed through. At that point, I had prayed out of and beyond self with no thought or concern of anyone else hearing me. I touched heaven and the God of heaven touched me.

With a perfect peace about everything including no thought about my finances I went back onto campus and to the library in study for exams. Somebody came for me. I was wanted on the telephone. That was unusual. I rushed to another building where there was a phone.

It was Pastor O. N. Todd in Birmingham. He asked how I was doing. I told him I was doing okay. Then he cut through all small talk with, "How are your finances?" I had to tell him. He responded with, "We are here in a church board meeting and they asked me to call you. We want to pay for your schooling for the rest of this school year."

Jesus told us to enter the closet of prayer, shut the door behind us, and the God who knows all secrets will reward us openly.

He did! He does!

That was great then! But guess what! It is great now! I am living it again! I'm wanting to sing, "My Faith Looks Up To Thee."

I challenge you in two areas:

1) Do more than pray, "Lord bless all for whom it is my duty to pray." Get specific. Pray for people by name and by need. Say more than, "Lord I thank you for all your blessings in my life." Remember and articulate specific blessings and answers to prayer.

2) Remember and live again prayers and answers of the past. Tell others. Write them down. They become re-activated. New ones are birthed.

Meditation is great! Do more of it! But it is time to go vocally active in personal prayer! Then expect God's open reward!

God's Norm, Miraculous to Us

As we re-align with God we regain increasing vision to recognize and expect Him in the now of our lives. Jesus Christ came to re-create God's best in us, for us, and through us.

I continue to be fascinated by some people's attempt to find what God's norm really is. God really wills and wants His norm in our lives. The appalling thing is that many people try in their own efforts, while not realizing their real hunger and need is what God is offering. Most of the time our human attempts end up in what is appropriately called "wreck-creation" rather than "re-creation."

Does it regularly occur to you that the Creator is also the Re-creator? Or, maybe the first question should be, "Do you really know Him as the Creator, your Creator?" - or is that just religious excess? Excess will not give access! Most excess was formerly alive but has now died. It will hinder, or even block.

God's Word instructs us to lay aside every weight, and sin that so easily beset us... Some of the weight is not just what is sort of sinful, but also the religious dead weight, excess. Some of the excess can become access when re-activated by the Holy Spirit, with the touch of renewed faith, into life.

Living, active, God-given faith cannot yawn while singing "Amazing Grace." Living, active, God-given faith will not be bored while reading or hearing John 3:16.

Sure, I know, there are "re-creational" activities other than singing religious songs, praying, and listening to preaching. On the beach I do not build pulpits out of the sand as I saw one preacher doing in a cartoon. Neither do I wear my suit and tie while working in the garden. In fact, I don't at many other places.

Sometime ago I heard someone say, "Get that smile off your face, you're supposed to be a Christian!"

Activities and associations not in alignment with God, even church activities, may rightly be called "wreck-creation." Activities and associations in sync with God and His ways produce "re-creation."

In the "re-creation" zone we have a Calvary-right to expect the miraculous. The miraculous should be so norm until we are surprised when miracles are not regularly happening, not just in "church gatherings" but in daily life where we "live, move, and have our being."

So, what about it? Let's have some "re-creation" around here when we gather! Then, let's experience "re-creation" wherever we go! Spirit-filled Christianity is not just a religion, you know. This is a way of life!

This, I believe, is God's norm for us, the miraculous!

You Saved, or Just Salved?

Salved? Then get the "L" out of it and be saved! But wait! Some mistake being salved with being saved. But being saved is more than simply getting the "L" out of it and pronouncing it differently.

Sure, get the "L" out of salve and it spells save, but being saved is more than the absence of. It is the presence of. In fact, it is the presence of, that enables you to enforce the absence permanently. That may help answer C.S. Lewis' aggravating question: *"If being a Christian is everything we say it is, then why are not all Christians nicer than all non-Christians?"*

Being saved is being born again. It is salvation, not religion! Being salved is being sort of soothed over with a touching story, even a Bible truth, especially in a religious atmosphere. It is temporary, nothing lasting, with no victory in heart and lifestyle.

Several years ago I tried preaching on getting the "L" out, in order to be saved. It was hard to preach and didn't go over very well either. I named some "Ls" to get out, like Lust, Lying, Laziness, Lasciviousness, and others.

Don't misunderstand. None of that devil stuff has a place in a Christian's life, but it takes the presence of Jesus Christ in His Love, and power to deal with the devil. Our Lord will also enable you to deal with human stubbornness and other misbehavior.

We are saved by confessing Jesus Christ as Savior and Lord, confessing our sins to Him, receiving Christ as Savior and Lord into our hearts and lives, and repenting of our sins and old life!

We are saved not by what we don't do, but Who we do know. We don't do or not do certain things in order to get saved, but because we are saved. We also serve the Lord not in order to get saved but because we are saved. It is sort of like you don't get up early and go to work in order to get employed but because you are employed. See?

Some get genuinely saved but fail to go on with the Lord. No one disciples them in the things and way of the Lord as the Bible says to do. They even get a good feeling with their new beginning but it fails. Get this. Some get saved and don't feel a thing immediately, but in faith follow Christ and the great feelings catch up later.

It is important that we all fully surrender our lives to God and also follow our Lord's instructions not to leave town until we are baptized in the Holy Spirit. That life newly emptied of sin then becomes filled with God's Holy Spirit! Being a Christian is not to be a vacuum.

Please don't settle for some kind of homemade religion. It won't satisfy, and the upkeep will wear you out. Sideline Christianity won't cut it either.

I heard and learned unforgettable things as a child. I heard an old preacher somewhat bluntly say, "Some people are just enough Christian that they can't enjoy the ways of the world, and yet have so much of the world's ways they can't enjoy being a Christian. They are just going to hell in a strain." I never sorted out all the theological status of that declaration, but Brother Isaac Jordan may have spoken more truth than fiction.

Go ahead for the real. Are you just saved? Get genuinely born again! Surrender to and identify with Jesus Christ. Be filled with the Holy Spirit. In the power of His person and life in you, get the "L" and a few other letters of the alphabet out of you. You will then not be left in a vacuum, but in the victory of your triumphant Lord in your life!

I'm Wrestling With Two "Appallations"

S orry about the new word. "Appallation" is not a certain mountain range. It is the state of being appalled. Here are my two "appallations."

I'm continually appalled at the things I wished I had said or done, and the questions I wished I had asked when there is no more opportunity to say, do or ask. Many times I had the nudge but ignored it until too late. He is now dead, she is now mentally incapacitated, or they have moved away and out of touch.

I'm continually appalled at the people who live drained and despondent because they think their lives have been wasted. I hear pastors wrestle with difficulties all because many, many people who have been helped, led to Christ, and blessed in so many ways never stop to let them know and simply say, "thanks."

I have others, but those are two of my big "appallations."

To want appreciation and camaraderie is not a weakness or fault. Jesus asked His disciples to watch and pray during His agonizing prayer in Gethsemane, but they chose to sleep. Jesus finally said to them, "Sleep on now…"

A poem I found years ago sort of says it. It is old and I don't know the author or even the title. Let's call it "Your Ministry to Friends is NOW." Here it is:

"If with pleasure you are viewing
Any work someone is doing;
If you like him, or you love him, tell him now.
Don't withhold your approbation (appreciation)
Til the pastor makes oration
And he lies with snowy lilies o'er his brow.

For no matter how you shout it,
He won't really know about it;
He won't know how many tear drops you have shed.
If you think some praise is due him,
Now's the time to slip it to him,
For he cannot read his tombstone when he is dead.
More than fame and more than money
Is a comment kind and sunny,
And the hearty, warm approval of a friend;
For it gives to life a savor,
And it makes you stronger, braver,
And it gives you heart and spirit to the end.

If he earns your praise bestow it,
If you like him let him know it.
Let the words of true encouragement be said;
Do not wait till life is over,
And he's underneath the clover,
For he cannot read his tombstone when he is dead."

~ Author Unknown

I dare you to begin replacing "appallations" with appreciations. You will be amazed at the lilt in life that comes to you as you give a lift of affirmation to others!

Where Awake? On <u>Your</u> Knees!

Samson was asleep on Delilah's knees. That's where he awoke. Read about it in Judges 16:19-20— *"...she made him sleep upon her knees."* Then *"...he awoke...and... the Lord was departed from him."*

About the time I was born, the preaching Presbyterian pastor, Dr. Clarence E. McCartney said of Samson, "A dangerous place to sleep, for out of that sleep none ever wakes but to weep. Out of that slumber men awake to find it is not morning, but midnight. And how dark that night!"

The place to awake is on <u>your own</u> knees, not another's. Awaking on another's knees, be it temptress, ill gotten gain, another's sacrifice, or hard earned inheritance, will not empower and energize you like winning on your own knees and the sweat of your own brow. If Samson, Judge (sort of prime minister) of Israel, had been on his own knees he would have had plenty of strength to withstand not only the temptress, but all the valiant might of the Philistines. He already had a winning track record.

The five Philistine kings of Gaza had kept miscalculating Samson's strength until Delilah's knees.

Japan miscalculated the strength and resolve of America when her fleet of planes attacked Pearl Harbor, but the peril of the Great Depression had not weakened America. It had brought her to her knees. Enough Americans had learned and experienced on their knees how to pray for the rescue of this great nation. The stories are replete of mothers and fathers, wives and children, brothers and sisters, and soldiers in battle, who on their knees with their valiancy, turned defeat into victory.

Judge Samson had become a backslidden Nazarite. From his mother's womb he was destined to deliver Israel, but the best ascribed to him was, *"He began to deliver Israel."* A Nazarite was to abstain from strong drink, and no razor was to come upon his head.

There was a law in Israel that no tool or instrument of iron was to be lifted above an altar. A Nazarite was a living altar to God and no shears or metal was to be over his head. The uncut hair was not the source of Samson's strength, but the sign of his pure devotion to God in his obedience. His disobedience led to the loss of his strength.

No impure alloy of metal shears denotes the pure devotion God is calling from every man and woman. He is calling for more than altar boys. Sir, you are an altar man. Ma'am, you are an altar woman. Pure connection with God without any alloy is what our Lord paid for, calls for, enables, and expects from every one of us. That may be what Floyd Hawkins had discovered when he penned in his song,

> *I've discovered the way of gladness,*
> *I've discovered the way of joy,*
> *I've discovered relief from sadness,*
> *'Tis a happiness without <u>alloy</u>'*...

Could it be that the sadness, confusion, and weakness of many Christians comes from the alloy above us, between us and God? Sleeping on the knees of another devotion, trust, allegiance, or source of comfort will deprive any of us of the strength that comes from the presence and joy of the Lord.

"The Philistines—the enemy of your life - lust, hostility, quarreling, jealousy, dissension, selfish ambition—be upon you, Samson, Bill, Henry, Mary, Jane, Sue, You—awake!" From whose knees will you now awaken?

How Long's a Mourners' Bench?

S ome call it a kneeling rail. Others call it an altar. There was a time when some called it a mourners' bench

A kneeling rail is where people kneel. An altar is where people are altered as they become a living sacrifice unto God. A mourners' bench is where people mourn, but more than just be sad. It is where, in sorrow for sin, people profess penitence. That means confessing to God, repenting, and experiencing freedom from that sin or sins.

I heard of one woman who felt convicted for all her gossip, and discord she knew she had caused. The pastor knew also. She went forward at an invitation and told the pastor she needed to put her "long tongue on the altar," the mourners' bench. Being the kind and tactful pastor that he was, he said to her, "Alright, very good. There is 40 feet of altar and if you need more we will provide that also."

So just how long does a mourners' bench need to be?

Really, it's not how long the bench, but how deep and how far do you need God's forgiving grace and healing love to reach in your life? God's mourners' bench reaches at least twice as far as your sins, or other needs.

God's Word says that you *"...have received of the Lord's hand double for all your sins."* In fact, just before that double provision was announced in Isaiah 40, the Bible says, *"Comfort, comfort my people..."*

Jesus declared, *"Blessed are those who mourn, for they will be comforted."(Matthew 5:4)*

Mourn. Comfort.

There are a couple of danger zones. One is when you reach the place that your sins no longer trouble, disturb, or bother you with tears of mourning. That's called gospel hardened, *"past feeling,"* no longer being convicted.

The other danger zone is when you are no longer bothered and heart broken over the sins and troubles of others.

Those dry and arid places in your life render you incapable of responding aright to God's voice in other areas of life.

Mourning that brings comfort is mourning that leads to Jesus Christ. That kind of mourning can turn your darkest days from sunset to sunrise; from gloom and despair to glory and delight!

So you prefer high praises and shouts of victory? Great! Then kneel and submit to God. Let your life be altered at the altar. Then be genuinely heart broken over every sin of commission and omission in mourning before God.

God's Word says of the Messiah in *Isaiah 61* that He will *"Comfort all who mourn."* To those who receive and follow Him, He said He will *"give unto you beauty instead of ashes, the oil of gladness instead of mourning, and the garment of praise for the spirit of despair."* Not only does the "Way of the Cross Lead Home," but it also leads to resurrection life now!

So how long's the mourners' bench? You decide!

Enlarge Your Faith Field: How

Sometime ago I got stuck with a zoom lens on my camera and needed to take pictures of some scenes up close. I couldn't. All I could get was a blur. Then someone introduced me to a wide-angle lens. It would reach pretty far out, but would give a maximum view of objects nearby.

Those view fields of the camera lens remind me of our faith fields. All of us have faith. The Book says so. But it surely does seem to me like the faith field of each of us varies in shape, size and function.

Some folks have a lot of faith to reach way out there and zoom in on distant things. Others have faith for all kinds of tolerance and acceptance in handling life today, but worry themselves sick about the tomorrows away out there. Some can believe God for one thing but cannot believe for another.

In fact, it certainly seems that some can believe God for big stuff but then stumble all over what appears to be little stuff.

The Bible says that each of us is given a measure of faith. I think what happens is this: Some develop their faith more and in different ways than others. Then when each tries to be a solo Christian they find loop holes, bubbles, and depressions where their own faith does not reach, and discouragement sets in.

Here is another reason we need one another. When you and I are in covenant then the combined faith field of both becomes the faith field of each. In a body of believers you can see very quickly how the total faith escalates into rapid expansion and effectiveness. Each contributes some that no other has and then each benefits from the total faith of all.

God is calling for an enlarged faith field in each life. As a result the faith field of your family, your church, your group will be raised and stretched to encompass whole areas beyond our normal capacity.

A pastor friend says he believes each church has a faith capacity. He said the church where he serves seems to have a faith capacity for about six or eight people to be saved each week, and six or eight are being saved. He went on to say that he is encouraging the people to stretch their faith to believe for more people to be saved each week.

Sometimes we draw unintentional limits around our personal lives and the life of the church by not recognizing the faith fields of others.

I challenge you to enlarge your faith field by letting it overlap another and another and in so doing, yours and theirs will all be greater. The combined faith of those with whom you connect then becomes the faith of each.

This combined faith is one factor that enlarges the faith field of a church and results in miracles in people's lives.

I guess what we need is a kind of zoom lens for our faith that will reach away out there and pull the promises for tomorrow up close, and at the same time give a wide enough angle to handle the whole spread of needs for today.

The same zoom lens faith that gives you hope and assurance for eternity, with a Biblical adjustment, will be sufficient for all your "now" needs up close. Recalibrate your faith that works for all the matters right around you and know that the way-out-there unknowns are secure in Christ also.

Let your faith and mine combine. That is the church, in Christ, redeeming one another!

Jim Gill, Marriage, & "Clamatized" Love

Jim Gill was one of my favorite people when I was growing up. He and Papa were good friends and spent a lot of time talking. Jim lived up the road from us on the main dirt road. We met the school bus up at his house and I've heard him use words I'd never heard before. Some I shouldn't repeat.

One time he shared with my father some of his wisdom on marriage. I can almost see him now. Jim was a black man, blind in one eye from an accident. There he stood with that blind eye squinted and a countenance of deep thought on his face. He said to Papa, "You know I didn't love Molly when we got married. We married and I got 'clamatized' to her later." We thought it was funny then, but now that I'm getting old I'm about to decide that old man was pretty smart. I'm sure that Jim meant "acclimated," adjusting to a new climate or different conditions.

I'm sure that if Jim had been asked if he loved Molly at the time of their marriage he would have quickly given a resounding "Yes!" He loved her with all he knew, but my, how his knowledge had grown with corresponding love. At the time of Jim's "clamatized" declaration, Molly had been confined to a mental institution for years and he had settled down to raising their three little boys on his 20 acre farm. I think that is love "clamatized."

Remember the story of Adam? You know, Adam in the Garden of Eden. He went into a deep sleep, and a unique wedding. When he woke up he was amazed, and I think he said, "There's a side of me I never knew before!" Adam was not the last man to marry, wake up, and make that discovery.

When that additional discovery of one's self is accepted and developed life finds awesome fulfillment! One day I walked into a building supply place wearing my "Fireproof Marriage" shirt with "I Love Marriage" across the front of it. A young man at work there stopped me. In a tone and expression of disbelief, he blurted, "Do you really think that?" With all the confidence I could muster, I blurted right back, "You'd better believe I know it!"

Marriage is a relationship governed by love and love is not static. If it was it would be brittle, would crumble, and fail. But real love works in the changing circumstances and conditions of life that enables the beginning love to grow and get "clamatized." I am still trying to learn, and practice what I am learning. Fortunately as an accomplished musician and music teacher Janelle is accustomed to a lot of practice and long rehearsals.

I took the challenge of The Love Dare, a Forty Day Journey to "Fireproof." It downright interfered with some of my schedules and plans, but there it is right in our Ultimate Guide, the Bible. One of the startling things I saw is the real consistency of God's way in marriage with Christian living at church, in the home, on the job, and in the marketplace. I already knew all that in my head but this was a refreshing refresher.

The other night Janelle and I were at the supper table, just the two of us. I improperly reached across the table, slapped my knife into the butter and tried to justify it with the excuse that just the two of us were here, so...After leaving the table it dawned on me just who the other person was and the place where we were! No guest and no place shall ever be more important!

I'm getting "clamatized," and I think it's more of my awakening discovery, love in action trying to grow up.

Bigger Pay for Bad News

Forty-nine years ago I picked up a second job to help support my preaching habit. My part-time work carried me into news gathering and reporting in radio and newspapers.

I worked about 25 hours a week gathering, writing, and reporting mostly bad news. As a pastor, I worked twice that much time studying, discovering and reporting mostly good news. I was paid $75 for the shorter time in bad news and $35 for double that time in good news.

At the radio station and the newspapers I was not asked to write and report on all the people who did not die, the cars that did not wreck, the houses that did not burn, and all the people who did not get arrested and jailed. The truth is, people were more interested in reading and hearing about the bad news.

Now, I must admit we did report births, weddings, and a few feature stories on someone whose success was remarkable so we remarked. People who knew and loved those people were about the only ones who would read and listen, but just about everyone would read and listen to the bad news. The media is in the business of selling news, and the most eager buyers are those who buy the bad. Keep in mind also that scarcity drives up demand and cost. Be grateful that bad news is still rare enough to make news.

Some people who merchandize bad news also help to make sure enough bad news is available. Some even deliberately get pictorial and word angles of others picking in their nose and quote words out of context to make it bad enough for the public. That may be why public debate participants will be pushed into poking a finger in one another's eye and fighting with accusations and divisive words.

The spirit of such bad news-slinging then spreads into epidemic proportions. Sometimes it spreads across the whole nation. OR, do the news sellers simply prey on what we the people demand?

Christians aren't immune or exempt. Like training our bodies to quit demanding junk food, it takes awhile to get information taste buds trained to quit feeding on misinformation, and our old appetites recalibrated to quit trying to live on junk.

I have an idea for a replacement of political public debates but space is too short here and John Q. Public's appetite will not yet pay for it.

Unbridled Christians loose on the range sometimes feed on less than the best forage.

Years ago some leaders in the church I was pastoring confronted me about my preaching. They convinced me I was not naming and coming down on sin enough; so I worked hard to comply. I missed. I came down on the wrong sins, theirs, so I was confronted again. I discovered those people wanted a sort of gladiator sport. They wanted to go to church to watch other sinners whipped and beat up. They could then report their findings to others who shared their carnivorous appetite.

Yep, the bad needs to be indentified and dealt with, but our Master Surgeon can wash away the sins without destroying the sinner. He removes darkness by giving light. He replaces despair with hope. He has taken on hell and offers you heaven. Christian, He invites us to go into business with Him.

In God's eternal currency Good News costs and pays more, but it is already paid in full!

BC Can Help
Overcoming Addictions

B C (Blessings and Consequences) can help a great deal in preventing addictions and go a long way in overcoming them.

I have been told from more than one reliable source that more than 100,000 people in this county of less than 400,000 are addicted. I don't know how specific those addictions are, but I assume it refers to anyone under the control of some substance or behavior that controls their lives and adversely affects the lives of others.

I first heard the word "addiction" when I was in the ninth grade. Mrs. Lee, our English teacher, found a magazine article in, as I remember, _Good Housekeeping_. She showed it to us and passed it around for us to read. I was stunned, shocked, and put on alert. It was about a teenager in New York City who tried marijuana, got addicted, and could not break free. His addiction kept calling for more, and the staggering cost led him to all kinds of illegal behavior causing devastation to his family and everyone around him.

I developed a mindset similar to the way I thought of playing with rattlesnakes, or handling un-insulated high voltage electric wires. I had already been taught at home and in church about BC, probably more about Consequences than Blessings. It was spelled out as h-e-a-v-e-n or h-e-l-l.

I already knew about nicotine and alcohol and their Consequences on people and families I observed. Nobody told me about caffeine until I got hooked. Fortunately that did not put any trauma on others, unless I ran out of it. That was dealt with immediately.

Now, here we are almost 60 years since that caring announcement by Mrs. Lee. Addictions are continually in nearly a third of our population. The money spent on purchasing substances and the cost of trying to curb and cure the victims is astronomical. Directly and/or indirectly money is taken from the pockets of everyone of us; and yet money is probably the least of the Consequences. I know families who have spent everything and gone broke trying to rescue one child, or one spouse. Some have then gone on to splitting, scattering, and experiencing the Consequences of the worst of pain, broken relationships for life.

I heard Dr. Lloyd Ogilvie, prominent Presbyterian pastor and later chaplain of the U. S. Senate, explain the biological change in a person's brain when they are born again. I then asked several born-again physicians their opinion about such a phenomenon. Each of those doctors agreed with Ogilvie.

The Bible gives to us repeated promises of BC in life. There are Blessings that accompany living above abusive behavior, and Consequences ascribed to not living according to God's redemptive plan.

BC alone can leave you in a devastating strait. Like Christ's Sermon on the Mount can be only a recitation of pious platitudes, BC can be just another declaration of good sounding but impossible dreams except for one thing.

BC gives motivation to make right choices, avoid wrong, and help cure, but it takes more. What more does it take?

Jesus Christ made possible His triumph over addictions in your life by His death, burial, and resurrection, and your acceptance of Christ and His provision by faith. I was told in a local rehab center that certain substances and behaviors cause little receptacles in a person's brain to open and multiply, demanding that particular substance or behavior and that if deprived of that demand long enough they will close and quit demanding.

I believe that just as surely as God creates a biological miracle in the brain at new birth, He can and will create a biological miracle of closing those addicted receptacles in the brain enabling the victim to walk in freedom if he chooses to! Hallelujah!

Go to God's Word and look around for BC! Use it! But it is no substitute for Calvary! Anchor in the death, resurrection, and life of Jesus Christ!

Jesus said, *"He whom the Son sets free is free indeed!"* *(John 8:36)*

A Place For Silent Saints

A number of years ago, I had a pastor friend who was over active and wildly vocal at football games, but placid, subdued and almost silent in worship at church. He and the church he pastored were restricted, fixed, and proper. I think I enjoyed the games as much as he did, but didn't have to make such a big ado about it. On the other hand, I got all excited at church and would become somewhat vocally expressive, but he may (though I doubt it) have gotten just as blessed, lifted, and totally helped as I did. He just didn't make such a big ado about it.

A person's behavior at a football game and behavior in worship at church have nothing to do with the right or wrong way of either. Well, maybe the cost, inconvenience, and duration of the time at one vs. the other may indicate a person's priorities.

Silent Saints? Maybe, but wait. Who are they?

People who are physically mute are thought by many to be silent, but they can be as Godly in their lives as anyone.

People who do not feel compelled to talk about everything every time anyone will let them, are considered by some to be silent.

People who will talk but who are not ready yet, are thought by some to be silent, but just wait.

People who could talk, and really have much to say, but won't, may be silent but only temporarily. Look out!

People whose spiritual gifting does not include proclaiming and declaring may be silent servers, but with cause.

People who have already spoken, become silent, yet their words and voice continue to speak in the ears and hearts of those experiencing their influence.

The vocal need the voiceless. Your spiritual fervor is not measured by your volume of sound or volume of words.

When the voiceless and the vocal blend, the silence is golden, and the vocal is punctuated with that silence into greater meaning.

We need each other.

There's a place for the silent saints and there's a place for the vocal. The truth is that none of us are wooden blocks or even robots. We are living recipients of God's grace capable of responding with shouts but never pouts, with silence but never shame. The Bible says we are living letters.

The person sitting at attention, visibly expressionless, and with a starched back may be worshipping or may be "in the flesh." Likewise the person sitting, standing, kneeling and dancing with vocal declarations may be worshipping or may be "in the flesh."

The big thing to know is that there is a place for the silent saints and there is space for the shouters. Let's just remember why we are silent and why we shout!

I have been told "impression without expression causes depression."

To Change or Not to Change

Change is a constant challenge in life. Change is neither bad, or good. It just is. Birth is a change; so is death. Life is in constant change. Yet there are unchangeables we must recognize.

Sometime back I was reading in Hebrews 12 where God's Word speaks of *"the removing of what cannot be shaken...that what cannot be shaken may remain."*

I glimpsed at the reality of my variableness. I seemed to hear anew in my innermost being, "God is the constant! From A to Z without Christ we can be shaken. From A to Z He cannot be shaken." So I asked, "From A to Z, what does that mean?"

Here's what I saw:

Your **Attitudes** can be shaken; but **His Answers** cannot.

Your **Biases** can be shaken; but **His Being** cannot.

Your **Commitment** can be shaken; but **His Character** cannot.

Your **Conduct** can be shaken; but **His Calling** is not.

Your **Development** changes; but **His Devotion** to you does not.

Your **Diversions** can vary and change; but **His Determinate Counsel** for you cannot.

Your **Energy** can go up and down; it can be changed; but His **Eternal Strength** is not changed, cannot be shaken.

Your **Faith** can be shaken; but **His Faithfulness** unto you is not.

Your **Grim View** can vacillate and be shaken; but **His Greatness** is not shaken.

Your **Gullible Appetite** for whatever comes by wiggling and glittering can change, but **His Goodness** is not shaken.

Your **Heinous Hopes** can change; but **His Holiness** does not change.

Your **Income** can change; but **His Infiniteness** is not going to change.

Your **Jokes** change; but **His Joy** remains for it's a fruit of the Spirit.

Your **Kind of Living** can change; but **His Kingdom** does not change.

Your **Loved Ones** will change; but **His Love** for you never changes.

Your **Morals** may change; but **His Mercy** is everlasting.

Your **Notions** can change; but **His Name** is the same yesterday, today, and forever.

Your **Outlook** can change; but **His Opportunities** for you never change.

Your **Plans** can change; but **His Power** is resident and secure in the Holy Spirit.

Your **Posture** can change; but **His Power** cannot change, cannot be shaken.

Your **Quirks** can change; but **His Quality** is always the same!

Your **Reasons** for serving can change; but **His Righteousness** is yesterday, today, and forever.

Your **Sins** can change (sins satisfied at one time quit and the sinner looks for others because none satisfy long); but the **Saving Grace** of Jesus Christ remains.

Your **Temptations** will change; but **His Truth** is not changeable!

Your **Understanding** can change; but **His Unfailing Wisdom** is unshakable!

Your **Variableness** is forever vacillating; but **His Veracity** is the same yesterday, today, and forever!

Your **Ways** change; but **His Word** is not shaken!

Your **Xpectations** change and disappoint; but **His Xcellence** never changes.

Your **Yielding** changes; but **God's Yearning** for you never changes.

Your **Zeal** changes; but the **Promises of Zion** remains the same in our Lord Jesus Christ!

This world order is shakable; but "God's Kingdom of Righteousness, Peace, and Joy in the Holy Spirit" is permanent, unchangeable!

Our God is in control! We can remain constant, unshakable, and secure in Him.

Behaving By Faith, or Fantasy?

There is a difference you know. Faith and fantasy are not the same. Sometimes they get scrambled and leave people frustrated.

Millions of sincere people pray for presidential elections. Some pray "republicanly." Some pray "democratically." Some pray their own biases simply reinforcing their fantasies. Some pray for an end to a war, and others pray for the financial mess to get resolved. Some pray for "righteousness, peace, and joy" in our nation and for leaders who will desire God's way and who will consult with God.

Is it possible for all the prayers being prayed to be answered as expected? Hardly. Could some of the prayers be for fantasies? Evidently. Could it be that prayers prayed in God's will by faith will be answered? Check the Book!

Fantasy is make-believe, wistful thinking. A person who fantasizes, imagining some desired thing, person, or event, pretends that desire to be reality. Fantasy almost always ends empty; at best temporary. Often it thrives on the sensuous. Fantasy feeds on what is not God's will, way or timing. God's will works through faith.

Faith is believing. It is substantive. It operates with evidence not yet seen. Faith is real. Faith is God-given and operates with His enablement. The Bible says, *"Faith is the substance of things hoped for and the evidence of things not seen."*

Many times people with a desire for something think they have used faith but have only fantasized or tried to exercise dead faith. The Bible says, *"Faith without works is dead."* Then when their prayer is not answered as expected they get disappointed and discouraged. That is the risk of praying to Father God who knows best, how and when.

Fantasy can come from multi-sources including a person's own selfishness, information or misinformation, or even the devil himself. Faith comes from God. It operates within God's will, God's Word, and God's Way.

The Bible says, *"If we ask anything according to God's will He hears us, and if He hears us we have the petitions we asked of Him."* Fantasy does not consult God's will, His Word, or His Way; or at least does not submit to Him.

When prayers and answers don't seem to match, there may be a need for a close review. Sometimes God's timing or method does not match ours and we check Him off early.

Most of the time in matters we pray about, God is up to much more than we imagine. Throughout the Bible, God works through the most unlikely timing and methods to accomplish His purposes.

Through whichever end of the telescope you choose to look, you will see life around us and across America in great need. We need a revival of righteousness. *"The Kingdom of God is righteousness, and peace, and joy in the Holy Spirit,"* the Bible says. Everybody wants the "peace and joy" but many reject the "righteousness." God's "peace and joy," the only real kind, are always accompanied with "righteousness." That means a right relationship with God and others. Peace and joy without righteousness is only fantasy. Faith includes and works within the embrace of righteousness.

Now is the time to trust God out of sight. Now is the time to pray daily in faith for God's direction in the life of each elected person locally and nationally. Be awakened and pray for the people of America that we be awakened. Could it be that the major financial crisis in America is right on the heels of the insidious attempt to remove "In God We Trust" from our money? Just a question!

God is calling us to cease our flimsy fantasizing, and Behave By Faith solidly as we experience "righteousness, peace, and joy in the Holy Spirit" across this great land.

Church, fellow believer, it starts with us!

Making a Good Marriage Better

It's okay for the unmarried to sneak view this also. I'd hope it would pass muster by a couple of unmarrieds, Jesus Christ and the Apostle Paul. People in the best marriages are the ones more likely to read it. I've noticed that those in the best marriages usually are the same ones who are most eager to make theirs better. They are also those who normally get along best with other people in life. There are exceptions. It still takes two to be married.

To make a good marriage better, both husband and wife must find and enter into more and more areas of agreement. Those marriages are made better when the Creator of marriage is made center. In the best of marriages it takes THREE to tango. Remember?

This is all about relationships. Marriage just happens to be the most concentrated and compact cluster of relationships anywhere. Relationships have a way of touching other relationships. They related. It is difficult to keep turbulence at home from spilling over into the work place, church, and about everywhere else. Likewise it is difficult to prevent problems at work, the church and about everywhere else from affecting the relationships at home. So take heed.

I never cease to be appalled at the little particles that infest and rip right through relationships.

Years ago a mouse got inside their house. Or, was it a rat? She said it was a rat. He said it was a mouse. After three days of pouting and quarreling, he finally said, "This whole thing is ridiculous," and he called for a peace treaty. She quickly agreed with, "You know I was thinking the same thing." They both laughed, made up, and settled in for the night. After going to bed she burst out laughing again. "I was just thinking how silly for us to make such a fuss over such a little frill of a thing." He responded, "You're right. I was thinking the same thing." Then she interrupted her giggles with, "But it was a rat wasn't it?" Guess the rest of that story. You guessed right. He didn't rest well on the couch for a week.

The three areas most people need the most help are also the same areas where people are the most sensitive, easily offended, and avoid getting help. The three? Finances, family and faith – resources, relationships and "religion."

I guess we all need to recognize we need help in order to reach out for help, or to accept help when it is offered.

In 1961 I was asked to serve with a handful of leaders in Conecuh County in putting on a Family Life Conference. That was in my early, early marriage before children so I felt competent to serve and I accepted. The Conference was first prompted by the local director of Department of Human Resources. We brought in experts from a long way off. We advertised about everywhere, invited everybody we knew, contacted people one on one, and then had sessions in different parts of the county for people's convenience. Guess who attended. You guessed it. A few families with strongest marriages and whose children were the best behaved were there. The primary ones DHR was trying to help were insulted by the very idea that somebody thought they needed help.

"How to Make a Good Marriage Better" is more palatable than simply, "Family Life Conference," or heaven forbid, "Help for Your Troubled Marriage." It is the title I borrowed from Dr. James Smith without his permission. He used to lead seminars by that title and he joined me on the radio each Friday morning for a thirteen minutes' interview on "How to Make a Good Marriage Better."

The fact that you have read this tells me you must have a high value on your marriage, an interest in helping others to "Make a Good Marriage Better," and that you want to better all your right relationships in life. Thanks!

Please Check Your
Gratitude Grid

Your Gratitude Grid separates that for which you are most grateful from that for which you are less grateful. Everyone has a Gratitude Grid but no two are exactly the same. In fact, expect yours to keep changing. I've been re-examining mine and adjusting it a little.

A grid is for separating some items from others. It can be a wire mesh with evenly distributed wires running in one direction perpendicularly crossed by another set of wires of even distribution running across them forming squares of an equal size. On the farm back home we discovered that wire flooring like that used for baby chick coops made an ideal grid for sorting dry peas from the husk. The peas in their dry pods were placed in a large cloth sack and stomped, or beaten with a pole. When the hulls were crushed and the peas loose in the sack, the contents of the sack were poured onto the grid.

The peas fell through the half-inch squares of the grid and the husk remained on top. All this began months earlier by turning the soil with a mule drawn plow, planting the peas, and hoeing the weeds and grass out. Finally, we were very grateful for the dry peas and bowed our heads in sincere gratitude at the supper table. We never made much ado at all over the husk.

My Gratitude Grid is getting re-calibrated.

I am concerned that in life there is priority confusion over the peas and the husk.

Recently somebody's polls reported that 69% of American people are dissatisfied with life in America. Dissatisfied is usually spelled u-n-g-r-a-t-e-f-u-l. What we need is an attitude of gratitude for what we have and where we are, all cradled in enough dissatisfaction with the status quo to motivate us to personally do something about it. America has the advanced medical, food, communication, health, transportation, housing, and recreation systems from the hearts and hands of myriads of grateful people who are making it happen. I've never paid enough taxes to pay my fair share nor have I personally done enough labor on any of the projects to make them happen.

My Gratitude Grid is getting more refined today.

I'll tell you something else. Today I am remembering just a little of the servitude of some of my ancestors to the McKenzies in Scotland and how Great, Great, Great, Great Grandpa and Grandma Andrew Jackson McGrath braved the unfriendly Atlantic and landed on the uncertain shores of this developing land. I am here today because of the sacrifices of unknown numbers of relatives and others before and during my lifetime.

My Gratitude Grid needs more adjusting than I realized!

My grandmother died a premature and miserable death from untreatable diabetes. I read that earlier caring and committed doctors dared to diagnose that disease by tasting the patients' urine for sugar. During my lifetime the progress has so advanced that it takes only five seconds for me to get a precise reading of my sugar level, and I know exactly what to do to bring that level right into norm.

My, my, my Gratitude Grid needs help!

I used to think it was a forever lifetime to reach 60. Now that time has briefly flown past me and here I stand at 72 with life's time and value in an inflation spiral. That brings me back to my Gratitude Grid. It has a vertical line to God and a horizontal line to others. It is called the Cross.

As I understand it this short side of life is but a speck. The full-length life is yet to come. That life, eternal life, begins now and opens into full blossom when this physical limitation ends. I understand eternal life is not measured only by length. Who wants our present state to be fixed forever as it now is anyhow? That's where our discontented satisfaction takes action.

Hold me down. I am about to shout!

America and the whole world is under conviction clamoring for something the world cannot give. The change the whole world is struggling for is to get right with God through Jesus Christ. Like Athens in the Apostle Paul's day, people are at the altar to an unknown god. Like Paul in Athens' day we are called to show and tell the world, including America, who that God is.

The better I know the God of gods, the King of kings, and the Lord of lords, Jehovah God as expressed in Jesus Christ, the more my total being - spirit, soul, and body - abounds in gratitude.

I think now I need a whole new Gratitude Grid!!!

The husk does not satisfy! Now check your Gratitude Grid. Find the peas! Toss the husk! Go ahead and give thanks! Our forefathers did!

Did You Get His Name?

Years ago a missionary in China told a lady about Jesus Christ and introduced her to Him. She was so excited and thrilled with her new discovery, but didn't remember Jesus' name. About a week later she went looking for the missionary. When she found him she told what had happened to her, but then she inquired, "Oh tell me His name again!" She had forgotten.

Did you get His name?

The angel said, *"...you are to name him Jesus, for he is to save his people from their sins."* But there are other people named Jesus. One Sunday a man named "Jesus" visited the church where I serve as pastor. He was a very nice man but he was not the Jesus I'm talking about here. The Jesus I'm talking about is Jesus Christ, Emmanuel, the Messiah!

We are calling out, "Tell Me His Name Again!" Each name and title the Bible gives Him further explains who He really is. His name is not neutral. There is power in His name. There is forgiveness in His name. There is healing in His name. There is deliverance in His name. There is hope in His name. There is life in His name. He is love.

"Oh Tell Me His Name Again!"

His name is Emmanuel, God with us! That's Him! In Him God is with us! How many believe that? I mean really believe it! He is Emmanuel!

His name is Jesus, Jesus the Christ! He now saves his people *from* their sins.

After the Chinese woman's request, "Oh tell me His name again," George Bernard penned these words and they were put to music.

> *They tell me of love's sweet old story.*
> *They tell me of a wonderful name.*
> *It thrills my soul with its glory.*
> *It burns in my heart like a flame.*
> *They say He's the one that so loved me,*
> *That in Heaven He could not remain;*
> *He came down to seek and to save me.*
> *Oh, tell me His name again.*
>
> *CHORUS: Oh, tell me His name again*
> *And sing me the sweet refrain*
> *Of Him who in love, came down from above*
> *To die on the cross in shame.*
> *This story my heart has been stirred,*
> *The sweetest I've ever heard,*
> *It banishes fear; it brings hope and cheer,*
> *Oh tell me His name again*
>
> *They say He was born in a manger,*
> *That there was no room in the inn;*
> *And in His own world was a stranger,*
> *But loved us in spite of our sins;*
> *They said that His path led to Calvary,*
> *And one day He died there in shame.*
> *He gave His great life a ransom.*
> *Oh, tell me His name again.*

They call Him the sweet Rose of Sharon.
They call Him the lily so fair.
They call Him the great rock of ages.
They call Him the bright morning star.
He's a prophet, a priest, and redeemer,
The king of all kings He now reigns.
He's coming in power and glory.
Oh, tell me His name again".

That's His name! You've got it!

A Call for Heart-felt Salvation

Is that the kind you have? Heart-felt?
The heart-felt kind does not make all heart-felt Christians "cookie-cut" identical, but there are some obvious similarities. Jesus was pretty clear about His new life in you. He called it being born again. It seems that something so defined would be very evident to the person experiencing it.

Being born is an "either you are or you are not" event. One psychiatrist said being born is the most traumatic event in a person's life. I don't know how he knows. I don't remember my first birth. Could it be that being born again is also somewhat attention getting? I do remember my new birth!

Sure, I know we are born again by faith! I also know that faith at work enables us to know, and know that we know without outside evidence. Join with me in knowing this: Redeeming faith, salvation faith, as real as it is, is not in insolation long before other evidence, like feeling, is birthed! That redeeming faith results in what I call "heart-felt salvation."

Is that the kind you have?

I've noticed that people who have heart-felt salvation enjoy basking in that reality! They begin developing heart-felt fellowship with other heart-felt Christians. More often than not people with heart-felt salvation begin entering into heart-felt worship. Listen. You will hear them in heart-felt prayer! It is even easier for people with heart-felt salvation to obey God in heart-felt evangelism and heart-felt care for others.

Too long at any one spot, or level, in a non-growth (static) place in Christian development can cause heart-felt salvation to revert back to little more than a mental assent or even a laborious duty with no anticipation for anything.

I've been told that in the natural, some people as they get older, lose their felt thirst when their body needs water. I'm learning to drink more water, sometimes not by feeling, but by faith according to my real need.

Could it be that people with heart-felt salvation, after awhile, without realizing it can become dormant in their responding to their Savior and even revert to a non-enjoyable life in Christ? Could it? Just a question.

I think so.

Does that mean their salvation is lost? Without quibbling over that, let me say this: It does appear that something you have and don't know it, could also be lost without ever knowing it.

But anyhow, this is a call to heart-felt salvation. I call it a "Christotonic." There is a "Christotonic" life Christ offers vs. a Platonic, "Aristotonic," or "Aunt Bea-tonic."

Platonic is sort of like a dry block of wood with no feeling. "Aristotonic" is somewhat Aristocratic, not allowing all believers to have equal access to God. "Aunt Bea-tonic" is a brief relief from your worries, and short lilts of friendship with others. It's the kind Aunt Bea and a handful of church women at Mayberry got from that new tonic they found until Andy broke it up.

Ah, but there is the "Christotonic!" The real tonic! That is the embodiment of Jesus Christ diffused into your total life – spirit, soul, and body – through the operation of the Holy Spirit in your redeemed life! **That's heart-felt salvation!** Is that the kind you have?

God's Call to the "Fast-Track"

This has little to do with trying to hurriedly get somewhere. Or, maybe it does!

Take note: Fasting has to do with two essentials in life – Food and God. I'm talking about Biblical-fasting, fasting and prayer. When you are full, especially over-full of food you have less space and desire for God. When you are full and running over with the awareness of God in your life you have less space and desire for food.

Everybody needs food. Everybody needs God. Some try to substitute one for the other, especially substituting food for God. Some substitute junk for food. Some substitute their ideas, things, events, and even some sort of religion for God. So they, of all things, try to fill their God vacuum with food.

Oswald Chambers once said, *"If Jesus Christ is not God, then the only God we have is an abstraction of our own minds."*

Fasting is a way of helping us subdue all substitutes and get to, or back to, the real with food and the real with God.

Regarding the why of unanswered prayers, Jesus told His disciples that prayer coupled with fasting is essential in those difficult cases. Then we run the risk of becoming problem-focused instead of answer-focused in Christ. Fasting must get beyond the gnawing focus on food and onto the hunger for God and awareness of His presence. Unencumbered God-given faith is activated to deal with any matter at hand.

In another place Chambers said, *"Think of the things you are trying to have faith for! Stop thinking of them and think of your state in God through receiving Christ Jesus...what marvelous strength you have in Him."* Then all the great blessings of God are not because of what you obey or what you do, but because of your relationship with Him. You obey and do the right thing because of your faith, rather than have faith and get God's answers because you obey and do the right things. We obey and do as a result of our relationship with God, not to cause a relationship.

We obey God in fasting and praying by faith in Him, then fasting and praying become evidence of our faith, not the cause. God's power breakthrough then follows the faith openly expressed in our obedience.

Fasting. I have noticed for sometime that my most perceptive time with God in prayer and study is between four and seven in the mornings. It dawned on me that is before I "break fast," call it breakfast. A few hours' fast is good, but I have discovered a several days' fast is much greater!

We should expect great breakthroughs in ways only God knows. Better than that, expect our personal and corporate hunger for God to be so increased and sensitized that no substitute will be acceptable.

Fast. Pray. Expect. Watch your real hunger for God grow and be fed! Then expect your real hunger for food to be more easily fed appropriately!

God's Fast-Track is the sure and quickest way!

My Doctor, My God, Alike?

Neither will do everything I ask them to do. In that way my doctor and my God are alike. I also believe both of them are alike in other ways. But here is my problem: I can't count on either of them to follow all my instructions.

Recently when I went to the doctor I asked the nurse if she would ask the doctor to call me each night about 10 o'clock and remind me to take that little pill he had prescribed for me. She indicated she would. When he came in I asked her if she had asked him and she said she hadn't. So I politely asked him if he would. He never answered me vocally. He just stared at me as if to say, "You have the prescription right there. Taking it is up to you." He has not called me a single time to remind me. I still forget to take that pill at night most of the time, but shouldn't he call me?

I asked my God if He would remind me not to have certain thoughts about some people, and if He would keep me from behaviors I later regret. He never did.

It finally occurred to me that I had the prescription right there in His Word, the Bible. He, God, has given me an open line to Him in prayer at all times. He has urged me to pray and not to give up. The more consistently I keep an eye on his prescription and talk with Him, the more reminded and strengthened I am to discipline my thoughts and actions.

Somebody reminded me again recently that "God does not give us our physical or mental habits; He gives us the power to form any kind of habits we like, and in the spiritual domain we have to form the habit..."

I formed the habit of taking that little pill every morning but somehow I guess it never became that important at night.

I have chosen mentors who have remembered and practiced following the instructions of their good doctor and their good God.

The Apostle Paul knew he had a part and responsibility in his walk with God. One Bible scholar interpreted Paul's words in *I Cor. 9:27 (RSV)*, *"I pommel my body and subdue it, lest after preaching to others I myself should be disqualified"*

When it becomes important enough to me, I will take my pill at night. I will follow my doctor's instructions instead of trying to get him to follow mine. When it becomes important enough to me, I will be more diligent in following my God's instructions instead of trying to get Him to change and follow mine.

In Philippians 4:5 God's Word says, *"let all men know your forbearance (self-control). The Lord is at hand." (RSV)* That means the Lord is present, so behave. I think that is more than a sign I read in the office of another pastor — "Jesus is Coming, Look Busy."

Years ago my doctor who was treating my diabetes asked me to have lunch with him. His presence made me so uneasy as I was selecting my food that day. I want to so live that neither the presence of my God or my doctor will make me nervous.

My doctor and my God are a whole lot alike. I'm learning that neither is my errand boy. I'm learning to discipline myself to follow their instructions without either of them having to tell me over and over and over.

Oops, it is 10 p.m. I must go take my pill. Oh yes, I also have a little note from my God in His Word and a matter that matters to Him.

PS. My God? My doctor? They are not one and the same.
- jsm

Universal Problem: Compulsive Generational Disorder

People continue to be perplexed by CGD – Compulsive Generational Disorder.

CGD is not a new thing. For a long time behavioral professionals have dabbled in it some and on occasions have identified some people's disorders as generational, coming from their parents and maybe grandparents or even further back.

I have a book that also identifies CGD as generational. In fact, it traces it all the way back to the first generation, our ever-so-great grandparents Adam and Eve. CGD gets its biblical name from Adam, called Adamic nature. Most who have read the Bible know CGD as SIN. It is generational. We all were born with it.

Remember? *"All have sinned and come short of the glory of God," (Rom. 3:23) "We all, like sheep, have gone astray, each of us has turned to his own way;" (Isa. 53:6)* and also, *"The heart is deceitful above all things and beyond cure, Who can understand it?" (Jer. 17:9)*

God does not make hopeless diagnoses. With every diagnosis He gives a solution. God's antidote to CGD is His ARO - Addictive Regenerational Order.

Don't let "addictive" throw you off. God's Word says of the household of Stephanas in I Cor. 15 (KJV), that they were addicted to the ministry (care) of the saints (others). Compulsive, uncontrolled, behavior is worse than addiction. Addiction is something found to be favorable compared to anything else that person has found until they find it irresistible. I'm addicted to brushing my teeth every morning. Sometime ago somebody asked me if I would be going to church the following Sunday. I answered with, "If I can't find anything better to do." I went. Finding a fulfilling way of life is addictive.

Not only have *"we all like sheep gone astray,"* but *"the Lord has laid on him (Christ) the iniquity of us all,"* and sure, *"the wages of sin is death; but the gift of God is eternal life through Jesus Christ our Lord."(Romans 6:23)* Oh yes, CGD – *if we say we have no sin we deceive ourselves and the truth is not in us (I John 1:8),* but hold on, ARO – *If we confess our sins, he is faithful and just to forgive us our sins, and to cleanse us from all unrighteousness (I John 1:9, KJV)*

Regenerational is what happens at "new birth" – born again, regenerated. Real regeneration transfers your generational possibilities from the first Adam to the last Adam, Jesus Christ. Substitutes always become less satisfying when the real shows up. Regenerated people are no longer obligated to be trapped into the disorder of those only generated. They are then free to choose order rather than be forced into disorder.

I found a note from my father written at least 51 years or as many as 70 years ago. I was awed by that little penciled note. He told me, "To have order, a man must be in order."

Think about it. See the connections between disorder in one area of your life and an accompanying disorder in another area. On the positive, notice the order in other areas of your life when order comes into a different area. When order comes into your spending there is more order in your available funds for necessities. When order comes into your eating there is more order in your physical well-being and sometimes in your finances. When there is order in your driving there are fewer traffic tickets and accidents. See what I'm talking about?

CGD – Compulsive Generational Disorder is corrected by ARO – Addictive Regenerational Order.

Don't Wash Your Net Yet!

"Fresh Bread" has a way of not being easily pushed off the table – "Don't Wash Your Net Yet!"

This "life-grabber" got me. It won't let go. It's still on the table, but not tabled. "Don't Wash Your Net Yet!"

I still don't know the full impact of that message. I know it leapt out and grabbed me. I could hardly determine if I should remain in the 'pulpit' – preaching posture – or go to a pew – chair. I'm sure this is for others.

"Don't Wash Your Net Yet!"

There it is in Luke 5 – empty boats and would-be-disciples washing their nets. Those professional fishermen, experts at their trade, were hanging it up. They knew their trade, knew the lake, and they knew the fish. They had fished all night, the boats were empty, and they were washing their nets. Quitting. For how long? We don't know. Evidently washing their nets was a procedural act. Jesus taught them for awhile and then told them to do it His way – launch out into the deep. They first objected but then obeyed.

I can almost hear Jesus saying "Don't Wash Your Net Yet!" Don't hang it up. Don't quit!

Could it be that some of us have been toiling all "night" in shallow water? Too many of us have been in the dark?

Just because it's always been done that way does not make it inviolable. Our Lord is the Light. Have we spent too much time and effort at night in shallow water?

"Don't Wash Your Net Yet!"

Here is what I am deciding:

Church, wherever you are, this is a right time for being the church that God has called us to be. This is not the time to "fish" in the "dark" like we may have been fishing and catching nothing.

This is the day (time) the Lord has made and He has matched us with this time.

"Don't Wash Your Net Yet!"

The Lord is nudging and really compelling me to forget about washing my net yet. I'm still waiting for more details from my Lord on what to do with "my net," I'm not washing it yet. Go ahead and mark it down. I'm not washing my net yet.

Expect a change or two. For one change I am determined to do less "fishing" in the "dark."

Expect by faith, go with our Lord's disciples in Luke 5 beyond your feelings and fragmented memories. When Jesus instructed His disciples to launch into the deep they remembered their fishless night, but in obedience Peter said, "But because you say so, I will let down my net."

He did. They did. The rest is history. What a catch!

Let's not wash our net yet! Let's just do it our Lord's way!

Moving From Denial to Peniel

This has to do with moving from the Desert of Denial to the Land of Peniel. Many never make the move.

Denial means rejecting what you should be accepting; saying "no" to a request or a demand when you should say "yes." Denial can be out of sheer ignorance. Often it is out of rebellion or just stubbornly rejecting some offer with peripheral excuses. Apparently Simon Peter denied Jesus for fear of embarrassment or personal endangerment.

Peniel is the name of the place where Jacob wrestled all night with whether to or not to obey God. He finally surrendered and, "called the place Peniel; because I saw God face to face, and yet my life was spared." *(Ecess. 32:30)*

Peniel, the face of God, – Moving from Denial to Peniel. Many people forever want the hand of God for a hand-out, but not the face of God for fellowship. Hell has sold a bill of goods to many, either saying or inferring that God is mean and out to do you harm. The ignorant and unlearned say things like, "Quit preaching to me!" Preaching, real preaching, is to show the face of God. It means proclaiming good news! Unfortunately those of us who preach have sometimes proclaimed condemnation. Instead of God's promise and provision to those already condemned we have sometimes declared your condemnation. Please forgive us!

Denial is a desert. To live there will dwarf and destroy you.

I have learned that God is omniscient, all knowing. I deny that truth when I behave and say things I would not say in His physical presence. Is He, or isn't He omniscient? To deny His omniscience by my actions puts me in a desert of denial and makes me a desert dweller. I'm not created for that kind of independent living.

Peniel is a land where I am aware of God's presence, a place of God's face, where my life is preserved.

After denying his Lord, Peter saw the face of Jesus, heard Him and wept bitterly. That short stint in the "desert" was too much for him. The sure presence of His Lord gave to Peter a Peniel experience. Peter re-entered the land of Peniel, a face to face experience with Jesus.

Where do you live - in the desert of Denial, or in the land of Peniel?

Peniel has been paid for. Denial can offer only disappointment. Peniel holds His appointment.

You can move from Denial to Peniel by, like Jacob of old, surrendering in your wrestling, confessing your dilemma and changing your "no" to God to a resounding "yes!"

I challenge you, somebody, to move from the Desert of Denial to the Land of Peniel! There is a miserable Christian somewhere reading this. God is calling you to go ahead and surrender. Move from Denial to Peniel in that drained area of your life. Call some friend, tell someone what you are doing.

The Problem Ain't The Staint

Y ou know, the "staint" glass windows.
To solve a problem, first know what the problem is. Many people are declaring solutions to the problem without ever identifying the problem. Others are forever going around declaring the problem, but are not giving a solution.

Now, back to "staint." Staint is a valid word. It may be a Southern Idiom or even an old English hold-over, but it is alright. Read on. Staint is the shortest way of saying stained, like spilt for spilled or turnt for turned.

Somewhere I read that during the Great Reformation several hundred years ago there were over-zealous church people who made some poor diagnoses of problems in the church. In their eagerness to correct the problems some decided the reason life had gone out of the church were because of the stained glass windows in the church buildings, so they went around bashing them out. That's what I read.

Why on earth didn't somebody stand up and holler, "The Problem Ain't The Staint?" It may have been their inability to articulate in advanced Southern English.

The "church" in North America is in trouble. Jesus said, *"I will build my church; and the gates (authority) of hell will not prevail against it." (Matt 16:18 KJV)* There are exceptions, but the "church," in general, of North America is in trouble.

Can we still say, "The Problem Ain't The Staint?" Or, have we indeed substituted the ornate and nicety of our buildings and programs to become a substitute for the real presence and power of the Holy Spirit?

Could it be that the real problem is even deeper and we have grabbed at fleeting temporary worldly debris in an attempt to stay afloat?

A newly converted woman in Samaria wanted to get it right so she asked Jesus where to go to church, where to worship. She knew that some insisted on Jerusalem and others argued for "here on this mountain." Jesus told her, in short, that she missed the problem altogether. He said it was not the place, but God is Spirit and they who worship God will worship Him in spirit and in truth anywhere.

Someone quoted or misquoted Billy Graham awhile back as saying the Holy Spirit could be removed altogether from the churches in America and 85% could carry on as usual never knowing the Holy Spirit was not there.

Is it really not the staint windows, but the sin staint and confused expectations of people?

Underneath the surface symptoms of the problem is a deep current of insatiable searching of human hearts for the real that no substitute has fulfilled. The mimicking and copying of the real does not satisfy. Artificial fruit has only a temporary appearance of the real. It doesn't even have the flavor of the real, much less the satisfying nutrition.

The staint glass? It may be the problem after all. The churches had staint glass windows where God used to move, therefore staint glass windows falsely advertised. Their presence announced the presence of God. So the Reformation zealots may have acted more like Jesus who cursed the fruitless fig tree.

You cannot determine the presence of God by the glitter or gold, the organ or guitar, the lighting or sound, the building name or location, or the staint glass appearance.

I have just read this quote from Oswald Chambers in a cherished book for my birthday, *"The characteristic of a man without the Spirit of God is that he has no power of perception; he cannot perceive God at work in the ordinary occurrences."*

The problem ain't the staint window, but the staint saint. God is right there! Look up!

Your Stimulus Package, Now What?

A lot has been said about a "stimulus package" recently. It is hard for me to know exactly what it is and how it works, so I'm not going there. However, I know a little about other stimulus packages.

Everybody has a stimulus package. Some are similar to others, but no two are precisely alike.

A stimulus is "something that rouses or incites to action." Sometimes it is a thought, sight, taste, smell, sound, or even a memory that calls for more stimuli and/or action.

The stimulus package I know about is any one or combination of stimuli at work in a person's life. What gets you going? That's a hint to identifying your stimulus package.

I think a stimulus package is sort of like a man with a loaded gun looking for something to shoot. He is stimulated to shoot that gun. Most any target, especially a moving one will do. A good hunter first identifies what game he is going after. He will load his gun with bird ammo or buck shot. He will not load his gun, pull the safety off, and just walk around enjoying or wrestling with the stimulus call. The stimulus must not be in control.

I think a stimulus package at its worst is sort of like a person with hormones dancing out of control, or to music and sights designed for an empty and disappointed end. At its best harmonious hormones will lead to fulfillment in life within God's design.

A stimulant is what stimulates or "temporarily increases the activity of some vital process." People in a hurry often get the reverse of their expectations. After the action they feel farther from their anticipated results than before, yet many forget and go right back trying substitutes again and again. For instance, alcoholic drinks, I've been told, are depressants, not stimulants.

Homemade and worldly acclaimed stimulus packages ultimately prove to be depressants. They create an immediate high expectation and then do not produce.

We as Christians need more than stimulus packages. We must know what the stimulant is. Is it money, sex, prestige, inner peace, a certain kind of house, a fulfilling job, a fulfilling marriage, family, a one night fling on the town, a revenge on someone, better health, daily fellowship with a good God...?

The stimulus package must line up with the stimulant in order to achieve the end result. Is it all in order? Will it carry you to where you know you want to go? Will it carry you to where God wills for you to go? You do remember that His will is the only way. Right?

I challenge you to take a look at your stimulus package. You probably cannot sort it out or even identify the total package.

You should be able to recognize the dominant stimuli. Then look again at your stimulant, your real values in life. Does your stimulus package line up with your real stimulant, your sanctified values and God's goal for you?

The stimulus package God has for you will line up with His stimulant. It will meet your real needs and the cost is high. He has already provided all He asks of you. That's your life, your abilities, and every good and perfect gift you have.

Your stimulus package, now what? Surrender to God's alignment and live!

Please Avoid Substitutes
for Substance

Relying on substitutes for substance has been a problem ever since. The whole economic scenario in America and in fact, the world, may have roots in the age-old problem of people choosing substitutes for substance.

Just a few years back one study showed that 53 million acres of land world-wide were used to grow "tobacco, coffee, tea, and grain for alcoholic beverages." That land could have been used to grow nutritious food. I wish they had not listed coffee and tea, but anyhow.

Many of those crops were subsidized by American taxpayers. In addition more taxes went to study the cure of diseases caused by those substitute products, and still more of our taxes went for campaigns to encourage people not to use the products.

At that time sociologists reported that the cost of social problems resulting from liquor consumption ran into billions of dollars. Then there were the personal and family heart-aches and distress among the millions of alcoholics and others addicted in some way. Add to that the thousands who died or were seriously injured in alcohol related traffic accidents each year.

People in the know recently reported that there are 100,000 addicted people in this county. The personal, family, and taxpayer cost is incalculable. All of this has to do with people choosing substitutes for substance in search of answers to life's real needs.

I'm bothered. In my opinion we are gorged, obese, and starving on substitutes while the substance of good land, right nutrients, and gainful employment are by-passed.

Could it be that dealing with substitutes that are pawned off onto the public for real substance can be an economic stimulus that will benefit financially, socially, and spiritually the total life of America?

I believe it could, but I also learned down on the farm that it is difficult to train foxes to safely guard the hen house.

So what do we do? Maybe each of us should check our own personal "substance cabinet" and see if some substitutes have gotten in there.

A young man up in the jail explained to me his substitute for an honest day's work didn't work. He got caught. The cost far exceeded his expectation for the stolen goods, and the benefit was sub nil.

Several years ago a friend decided he would substitute another woman for his wife. He did. After awhile, in great distress, he called me. The substitute was far too costly and the expected benefit never arrived.

An 18 year old had a one-night fling, a substitute for God's way. Her cost was high – it cost innocence, untold family expenses, AIDS, and early death!

There is no substitute for substance. The One who designed and created us knows best how we function. We cannot improve on His plan and His way.

Come a little closer. Some substitute their experience with God for God Himself. Their testimony stands taller than their Lord. Others substitute their church for their Christ.

Some substitute God's gifts to them for the God who gave them the gifts.

Substitutes look so real and reasonable, but God's Word says, *"Faith is the substance...." (Heb. 11:1 KJV)* Substitutes will all vanish, but Faith anchored in God with His eternal provision is forever.

Please, in all circumstances, avoid substitutes for substance!

Over My Head? Not My Head!

Sometimes I have to be told the same thing more than once, and sometimes repeatedly before I get it. Fortunately I wrote it down the last two times. I think I'm about to get it.

It has to do with what's over my head. Is it, or is it not?

Several years ago I lamented that all of life seemed to be over my head. I whined about various responsibilities that were just too much for me. On and on I went. I'm still not sure what I wanted anybody to do about it. I don't like sympathy. I didn't even want people to think, "Poor Joel."

Then sometime later it got to me again. I remember turning my prayer into a whining session with God. I actually blurted it out, "Lord, I'm over my head!"

I think now that when I whine things to God that I'm apt to be trying to put the blame on God. Well, recently I was at it again.

Have you ever felt you were into something over your head? Then you know what I'm talking about.

A responsibility there…

Somebody's need here…

The expectations of others yonder…

A sense of inadequacy…

The unfinished work of yesterday…

The continuing rush of tomorrow…

The fast fleeting moments of today...
The unreached goals of the years...
And on and on and on...
Even in a prayer it was hard to find an appropriate position. Standing wouldn't do it. Neither was sitting. Kneeling seemed too much like submitting. Walking worked for a bit. Finally I found myself just wallowing, but not so much in prayer as in self-pity.

I went back and read what I wrote the last time I felt I was overwhelmed. I was going through a whole re-enactment. I think my Lord was standing there with His arms folded, a great big "I-know-something-you-don't-know" smile on His face, and a caring sparkle in His eyes.

"Over your head?"

"Yes Lord, over my head!" I repeated!

Here's what He gently, calmly, and assuredly said, "I AM YOUR HEAD."

In my awakened state I quickly recalled His speaking it to me earlier. Read it in Ephesians 1:17-23 which concludes with,

Now He is far above any ruler or authority or power or leader or anything else—not only in this world but in the world to come. God has put all things under the authority of Christ and has made Him head over all things for the benefit of the church. And the church is His body; it is made full and complete by Christ, who fills all things everywhere with himself. (NLT)

Isn't it amazing how much fret and over headedness we could spare ourselves just by reading and believing God's Word, the Bible?

Over my head? No! Not my HEAD!

The Resurrection is Not Over

Often one week after Easter, Christians feel a big let-down. The epoch celebration of the bodily resurrection of Jesus Christ is in past-tense. What can be done for an encore?

What a day it was then when Christ came out of the grave! Christ arose! The created world went into convulsions with earthquakes and an eclipse of the sun. Saints of old got out of the graves and walked the streets of Jerusalem! Those phenomena are not perpetually repeated, but the reality and effects of the Resurrection are!

Wow! What a day in local churches on Easter morning! The sanctuaries are full of people. People enter into worship by praying and hearing God's Word! Believers lift their voices in song! Choirs excel themselves! God's Word is proclaimed with anointing and clarity! People are born again! Backsliders return to the Lord! People experience God anew!

A couple of days after last Easter I tried to write something about "Post Resurrection Assurance" but it wouldn't write. Post Resurrection? There is no such thing! Our Lord is still risen. He is still alive! The Resurrection is still on! God's Word declares that, "Those who come" to God must believe that He **IS**, and that He **IS** a rewarder of them that diligently seek Him." (Heb 11:6 KJV)

God, in Christ, is!
Everything about Him is!
Creation is!
His crucifixion is!
Redemption is!
His love is!
Forgiveness is!
Healing is!
Deliverance is!
Hope is!

Everything in Him that ever has been is! Then, materially and historically, His empty tomb announced forever that His Resurrection is!

More than materially and historically, His Resurrection is evidenced in personal lives who surrender to the crucified, risen Christ. In that surrender, believing that He is, and is a rewarder, diligent seekers are still discovering His Resurrection not to be a post event, but a present happening!

As real as God's creation and procreation are still happening, so are His Death and Resurrection still operative in those who believe! Got anything going on against God's will and way that needs to die? His extended Crucifixion is available and transferable to you! Got any Resurrection needs? Our Lord's Resurrection is available and transferable to you!

Post Resurrection? Never!

The risen Christ is present in worship again the week after Easter equal to Easter Sunday, and every time people meet. Am I equally receptive? Are you?

Today's Message:
More Than Merry

S inners and saints sing. They also laugh and cry. Both do both.

Some seem to think that being a Christian is a joy-killer, a sentence to boredom, total sobriety and only serious sauntering around. They, by their own definition of "Christian," easily identify anyone professing to be a Christian and not fitting their grid as a hypocrite.

Others think that being a Christian is an extended trip of merriment, a sustained hype, total festivity, and living in giggly denial of the real pains and issues of life on earth. They especially think that corporate worship is limited to excitement, and question the genuineness of anyone's real faith if they do not outwardly fit through that grid.

Probably no one reading this is locked into the extreme of either of those grids.

We should hear God's message: MORE THAN MERRY!

We should hear God's message: MORE THAN MOURNING!

Merry: Jolly, full of fun, laughter, pleasant, favorable, and agreeable.

Mourn: To feel or express deep sorrow or grief, lament, heartbreak.

Here's a call to listen with both ears. There's a time to be merry! There's a time to mourn!

This is a time to recognize two ditches, one along each side of the same road. Neither ditch is good traveling. Both ditches are valuable. The road is where to travel. God's Word says there is:

"A right time for birth and another for death,
A right time to plant and another to reap,
A right time to kill and another to heal,
A right time to destroy and another to construct,
A right time to cry and another to laugh,
A right time to lament and another to cheer,
A right time to make love and another to abstain,
A right time to embrace and another to part,
A right time to search and another to count your losses,
A right time to hold on and another to let go,
A right time to rip out and another to mend,
A right time to shut up and another to speak up,
A right time to love and another to hate,
A right time to wage war and another to make peace."
Ecclesiastes 3:2-8 (MSG)

Read Luke 12:19 also. The shortsighted worldly person is portrayed.

"The farm of a certain rich man produced a terrific crop. He talked to himself: 'What can I do? My barn isn't big enough for this harvest.' Then he said, 'Here's what I'll do: I'll tear down my barns and build bigger ones. Then I'll gather in all my grain and goods, and I'll say to myself, Self, you've

*done well! You've got it made and can now retire.
Take it easy and have the time of your life."*

*"Just then God showed up and said, 'Fool!
Tonight you die. And your barnful of goods—who
gets it?'*

*"That's what happens when you fill your barn
with Self and not with God."* (MSG)

More than merry! More than mourn! Know God's Word,
and have faith enough to trust God! Live!

Gardening:
Pole Beans and People

People living outside the garden miss a lot! Ask the Adams' family. You know, Eve and them.

It is now gardening time. This is for people inside and outside the garden. After all, those outside the garden eat out of the garden.

Beans—I personally know about butter beans and string beans. Both come in a bush variety, and a pole variety.

The bush variety is grown on a small bush-like plant close to the ground. Short people with long arms are best for picking the bush beans.

The pole variety of beans has nothing to do with pole-cats, the South Pole or people from a certain country. Pole beans climb poles up to head high and higher. They sometimes are called running or climbing beans. They produce longer, produce more, are easier to pick and better to eat. The troubling snare we had was acquiring the poles and getting them properly into the ground for those beans to climb on.

When I was a boy there seemed to be a shortage of "manual" labor so guess what? They tapped in on "boyual" labor. Without a doubt the most dreaded job Robert, my brother, and I had to do was to stick pole beans.

We had constant conflict while cutting slender sassafras trees in the woods and dragging them to the garden for sticking the beans. We used an old steel buggy axle to pound into the ground making a hole by each bean plant. A sassafras pole was firmly anchored in each hole for the beans to climb on. Then to top it all off we had to go back repeatedly and help some of the beans find the pole. Then they would climb right to the top.

I promised myself over and over that if I lived long enough to grow up I'd never plant those forbidding pole beans as long as I lived. We would live poles apart. Then sometime ago Janelle requested that I plant pole beans in our garden. I forgot that ancient promise, and planted. When those pole beans started growing my memory came right back.

I cordially invited Janelle, a non-gardener, to the garden with me. She went. She was amazed. I was appalled. Bean vines were wrapped around corn stalks in the next row. Some were entwined around old sticks on the ground. Others were twisted into gnarled knots of ingrown entanglements. They had attempted to reach upwards but with nothing to hold onto they simply wrapped their little scouting tentacles around themselves, vine and all.

I walked away with something bigger than beans. I met God in the garden that day in a way I could not have met Him outside.

People are a lot like pole beans. We have a God-given inclination to reach up. When we fail to have a meaningful relationship with God, like climbing pole beans, we reach for all kinds of alternatives.

Some people wrap themselves around things. Some wrap themselves around other people. Some become entwined around themselves.

We are climbers. Our created inclination is upward. Somebody else's stalks on another row won't cut it. Ground level debris leads to nowhere. Living only for ourselves will leave us in knots. Just any old stick won't do.

We are not "bush" people or "stick" men. We are climbers! Our created inclination is upward. The "pole" the Son of God used to give us stability and direction upwards is the cross.

Any overwhelming tempt or attempt to wrap ourselves around any alternative may be that our reaching tentacles missed the cross. Inside the garden God has gardeners to help us. We were born to climb upwards. We? You and me!

The Fence for Better Defense

L ife experiences as a boy back on the farm keep providing vivid helps in my life and some of the help I share with others.

We had more than four miles of fences, most of which were in constant need of fixing. That means repair, mending, replacing posts, and constant surveillance. There's a whole lot of that in life.

Sometime back, I was trying to help someone who was finding it difficult to stay in his own yard regarding moral behavior. What do people do with such issues? Call out to God and put it into His hands? Then just do whatever they feel like doing since it's in God's hands?

Maybe it can be answered this way. Since your car registers 120 mph on the speedometer and may be capable of going that fast, is it okay to drive at any speed anywhere up to that maximum? Of course not. The powers that be have determined rules and regulations for your safety and the safety of others, as well as the well-being of that automobile.

That's sort of like it is in life. God our Creator knows our capabilities, but He also has determined rules and regulations for our safety, the safety of others, and the over-all well-being of our personal lives. We find those guidelines in the Bible, God's Word. Yet we are responsible for knowing and obeying or disobeying. We also are recipients of the rewards or consequences of our chosen behavior.

Now, back to "de fenses," I mean the fences. We had rail fences, picket fences, board fences, barbwire fences, chicken wire fences, and hog wire fences. The following fence-help I've given others has to do with the proper posts. This I've given to others but also have used myself. In fact, no fence is stronger than its posts.

First, select good strong, stout corner posts. I recommend:

The Following Four Corner Posts:

1. Know what God's Word, the Bible, says.
2. Pray according to God's will and His way.
3. Believe and picture yourself morally pure.
4. Keep yourself accountable to someone.

Between the corner posts there must be secure and reliable line posts. I recommend:

The Following Eight Line Posts:

5. Avoid concentrating your thoughts on the wrong behavior, and replace with right thoughts.
6. Control your eyes, speech and hearing.
7. Control and avoid situations of being alone with.
8. Avoid sensual talk, even humor.
9. Avoid inappropriate touch.
10. Avoid being overloaded in other areas of your life.
11. Avoid getting obligated to or getting another obligated to you.
12. Learn how to say, and say, "No" or "Don't" and replace with a pure "Yes" to right.

These are 12 posts. Posts alone on a farm or in a person's life do not make a fence. However, broken, rotten, or missing posts guarantee no fence. God will enable you, but without you He will not automatically put and keep these posts in place. No amount of promises, commitments, or resolutions can hold up without good posts.

Any humans reading this - please mull on it and fence these posts with prayer and surrender to Jesus Christ.

On the farm someone said the fence must be "horse high, bull strong, and pig tight." In our lives our best defense begins and ends with a right relationship with the Christ within. All the posts, promises, commitments, and resolutions are then anchored in Him who enables us to overcome the world, the flesh, and the devil. Still not sure? Get off the fence!

LaVergne, TN USA
14 October 2009
160873LV00002B/56/P